Dangerous Lunatics

Dedicated to
Dr. Stephen Setterberg
*

In admiration of his visionary advancement of
depth psychology

Brett Kahr

Dangerous Lunatics

Trauma, Criminality, and Forensic Psychotherapy

Published in 2020 by Confer Books, London

www.confer.uk.com

Registered office:
21 California, Martlesham, Woodbridge, Suffolk IP12 4DE, England

British Library Cataloguing in Publication Data. A catalogue record for this book is
available from the British Library.

ISBN: 978-1-913494-06-3 (paperback)
ISBN: 978-1-913494-07-0 (ebook)

Typeset in Berling by Bespoke Publishing Ltd.
Printed in the UK by Ashford Colour Press.

Books by Brett Kahr:

D. W. Winnicott: A Biographical Portrait (1996)
Forensic Psychotherapy and Psychopathology:
    Winnicottian Perspectives, Editor (2001)
Exhibitionism (2001)
The Legacy of Winnicott: Essays on Infant and Child
    Mental Health, Editor (2002)
Sex and the Psyche (2007)
Who's Been Sleeping in Your Head?: The Secret World
    of Sexual Fantasies (2008)
Life Lessons from Freud (2013)
Tea with Winnicott (2016)
Coffee with Freud (2017)
New Horizons in Forensic Psychotherapy: Exploring
    the Work of Estela V. Welldon, Editor (2018)
How to Flourish as a Psychotherapist (2019)
Bombs in the Consulting Room: Surviving
    Psychological Shrapnel (2020)
Celebrity Mad: Why Otherwise Intelligent People
    Worship Fame (2020)
On Practising Therapy at 1.45 A.M.: Adventures of a
    Clinician (2020)

"There have been at all times, and will be, hordes of predatory parasites who infest and infect the community. They hover on the outskirts and prey on the fears and helplessness of the more exposed and feeble members; or they penetrate into the vitals, and twine like the taenia in the very track and trail of nutrition and strength; or they insinuate themselves, like the cysticercus, into the very brain. They live upon the life of others."

(Anonymous, "Dangerous Classes", *The Medical Critic and Psychological Journal*, 1863, Volume *III*, p. 137)

"Wenn du einen Menschen tötest, hast du die Welt getötet, wenn du einen Menschen erhälst, erhälst du die Welt …"
[If you kill a man, you have killed the world; when you support a man, you support the world …][1]

(Talmudic saying, from the Sanhedrin tractate, devoted to civil and criminal proceedings. Quoted in Belke, 1978, p. 79)

Contents

INTRODUCTION
The Man Who Shot His Mother And Father In The Face

Nihil Ammiano praeter aridam reſtem
Moriens reliquit ultimis pater ceris.

(Marcus Valerius Martialis [Martial], "De Ammiano ad Maronillum",
Epigrammata, c. 86 CE – 103 CE, Liber Quartus, LX [*sic*])

[When Ammianus' father breathed
His last, his son, hovering in hope,
Found that the final will bequeathed
Him nothing but a length of rope.]

(Martialis, 1773, p. 83; Martial [Martialis], 1973, p. 81)

Nearly forty years ago, I first set foot on the back wards of a battered, bedraggled psychiatric hospital, tucked away on the outskirts of a tiny village in the remote English countryside. As a very young and extremely inexperienced psychology trainee, my knees literally trembled with fear as I walked through the locked doors of the psychogeriatric unit which housed hundreds of chronic, severely mentally ill patients, most of whom had received a diagnosis of schizophrenia. Within seconds, I became nauseous from the horrific odour of the urine-stained and faeces-smeared carpets, not to mention the morbid stench of the omnipresent cigarette butts spattered all about. Unsurprisingly, I began to retch.

The long-serving and somewhat jaded Consultant Psychiatrist – immune to the ghastliness of the physical surroundings – welcomed me warmly into this hellish environment and suggested that I should begin my apprenticeship with a tour of this nineteenth-century institution. Naively, I assumed that my new boss would escort me round personally; instead, he explained that my tour would actually be conducted by none other than "Fred", one of the oldest patients on the ward, who knew the layout of the hospital better than any of the members of staff.

Within moments, Fred appeared, as if by magic, and shook my hand most graciously. He smiled with tremendous enthusiasm: "So, you're the new psychologist. It's a pleasure to meet you." Fred chatted breezily and did not seem to be schizophrenic at all – quite the opposite, in fact. Only 5' 1" in height, he struck me as somewhat childlike, especially as he spoke in rather a high-pitched voice. Certainly, from a physical point of view, this patient did not seem frightening in the least.

Fred then marched me through the dank rooms of the cavernous hospital and, afterwards, escorted me into the surprisingly well-maintained gardens. He chirped, "To your left, Brett, well, that's the infirmary, for patients who need medical treatment. And just beyond, to your right, that's the hairdresser's hut, where some of the old ladies go for their curlers. And over there, beyond that tree, that's the gardening shed." Fred spoke clearly and calmly and with great attention to detail. After an hour, we returned to the ward, whereupon Fred kindly offered me a cup of tea.

Although I had visited psychiatric institutions previously, as part of my training, I had never met a patient as sweet as Fred. He appeared to be incredibly sane and chipper, so much so that I actually wondered whether someone had made a dreadful mistake by having incarcerated him under the Mental Health Act 1959 all those many years ago.

At this point, the Consultant Psychiatrist reappeared and took me into his tiny office, strewn with stacks of dusty files, and asked me whether I had enjoyed my special tour. I told him that I had found Fred to be rather informative and, also, quite charming to boot. The psychiatrist seemed unsurprised by my description. And then, he quizzed me: "So, Brett, if Fred is such a lovely man, why do *you* think he has been a long-stay patient at this hospital?"

Nervously, I spluttered a grossly inadequate reply and expressed my deep uncertainty as to the reason for Fred's incarceration.

The consultant grilled me further: "Is he, in your estimation, a classic schizophrenic?"

"Well," I replied, "I failed to observe any obvious signs of either hallucinations or delusions or, indeed, of disordered thought."

"You are correct," he replied, "Fred is not *obviously* schizophrenic."

"But if he does not meet the diagnostic criteria for schizophrenia," I queried, "what has brought him here as a patient?"

The Consultant Psychiatrist beamed with a certain arrogance, knowing that I would never guess the real reason for Fred's incarceration. He smirked and then explained, "Many years ago, Fred took a handgun and shot his father in the face at close range, and then he shot his mother in the face, also at close range. Would you ever have suspected that such a small and seemingly unthreatening man could have committed the ultimate double murder?"

My jaw dropped in utter astonishment. Although I had spent only a brief time with Fred and had enjoyed his walking tour, I had not detected any sense of danger or madness. Fred seemed like a kindly old man. I would never have supposed him capable of either patricide or matricide.

Clearly, my education in psychology had only just begun. And before long, I came to realise that one cannot always identify a murderer on the basis of physical appearance alone or, indeed, as a result of merely one hour of conversation. Although some killers *do* look completely deranged, with fire in their eyes and spittle drooling from their mouths, others, by contrast, appear quite placid and even gentle. I would have much to learn about the field of forensic mental health, namely, that branch of modern psychology devoted to the study of psychopathologically troubled individuals who perpetrate violence.

Mad people have committed offences – often grotesquely sadistic crimes – since the very dawn of time. Nowadays, we refer to a perpetrator such as Fred as a "forensic patient" – a mentally ill individual who commits an act, or acts, of deep cruelty. But, back in the nineteenth century, physicians would describe such a patient, somewhat more poetically, as a "dangerous lunatic" (Clarke, 1886, p. 88; cf. Theobald, 1924; Prior, 2003; Shepherd, 2016).

Now, within the very first hour of my very first day of employment, I had met my very first dangerous lunatic. And, as the years unfolded, I would, in due time, come to meet many more: murderers, paedophiles, arsonists, rapists, and thieves.

Given that most of us manage to navigate our entire lives without ever shooting another human being in the face, or raping a child, or burning down a building, or breaking into someone else's home in the middle of the night, why on earth should these dangerous lunatics do so? Perhaps these individuals suffer from some sort of brain disease or, perhaps, they might simply be rotten eggs, cursed by the Devil. What aetiological factors actually contribute to the development of such terrifying forensic illnesses?

And how should we deal with these people once the police have apprehended them? Should they be sentenced to a lifetime in a maximum-security pris-

on? Should they be incarcerated in perpetuity in a
special psychiatric hospital? And for those who do
become institutionalised, should we simply let them
rot in their cells or on the wards, or might we dare to
offer some sort of humane psychological treatment
in the hope of improving their quality of life and
thus contribute to the reduction of the possibility of
reoffending in future?

What, if anything, can we learn about the causes
and treatments of dangerous lunacy from the work of
our historical predecessors and, also, from our more
contemporary colleagues within the field of forensic
mental health?

Let us consider the case of a nineteenth-century
lunatic, "William B.", from Swansea, in Wales, who
had committed many acts of viciousness during his
lifetime. This Welshman embarked upon his criminal career by torturing and killing animals: fowls,
doves, cats, and dogs. In fact, on one occasion, he
actually cut the throat of a horse. In time, William
B. began to harm human beings as well; indeed, he
even stripped a younger sibling of his clothing and
then beat and scratched the boy's body, threatening
death. In due time, this dangerous man progressed

to acts of sexual violence as well as strangulation of a baby (Tuke, 1885). He even attempted to castrate an imbecilic inmate. In 1886, after William B.'s incarceration in the Asylum for the Insane in Kingston, Ontario, Dr. Charles Kirk Clarke (1886, p. 85), the Medical Superintendent, reported, "he can not recollect the time he was free from the desire to torture and kill." Unsurprisingly, such acts of viciousness forced Dr. Clarke (1886, p. 88) to diagnose William B. as a "dangerous lunatic".

According to traditional psychiatric theory, not every perpetrator of violence fulfils the diagnostic criteria for mental illness. For instance, when, in 1945, the crew of the American aircraft *Enola Gay* dropped atomic bombs on Hiroshima and Nagasaki, murdering more than 100,000 people and irradiating countless others, no one had ever suggested that those airmen should be institutionalised as dangerous lunatics. But many criminals do, unquestionably, suffer from dangerous lunacy, broadly defined. Indeed, in the mid-nineteenth century, Dr. John Purdue Gray (1857, p. 119) of Utica, New York, a physician who had studied nearly 5,000 cases of homicide over a period of fourteen years, concluded that, "A disposition to violence is a common characteristic of mental disease." Certainly, we know that madness and criminality often coexist rather intimately, as many overtly or covertly mad people will perpetrate violence and many perpetrators of violence will often be quite mad.

This short book concerns "dangerous lunatics": men and women, and even children, who commit crimes, invariably under the influence of extreme psychological distress. In the pages which follow, we shall begin by exploring how our predecessors mistreated dangerous lunatics across the ages, often subjecting these individuals to the most shockingly violent forms of punishment. We shall then consider how, for many years, most health care professionals dismissed criminality as little more than the consequence of degenerative brain disease. Thereafter, we will investigate the radically pioneering contributions of Sigmund Freud and his fellow psychoanalysts who dared to research the childhood histories of offender patients, often revealing that these individuals had suffered profound early traumata.

Having thus examined the field of forensic psychology in historical perspective, we shall then study two types of gross offending behaviour in particular, namely, paedophilia and, also, murder, through a psychotherapeutic lens, considering what we have come to learn about the deeper, unconscious origins of these extreme forms of sadism. We will conclude this study with an examination of the current state of forensic psychotherapy, exploring how those of us who work in the field of mental health might develop a more humane stance towards the treatment of perpetrators in years to come.

Torture and execution:
ancient remedies for perpetrators

*And where th' offence is, let the great
Axe fall.*

("Claudius King of Denmarke", in William Shakespeare,
The Tragedie of Hamlet, Prince of Denmarke, c. 1599 – 1602,
Act IV, Scene v, line 244)

Throughout the course of human history, men and
women have committed grotesque acts of deep criminality. One need but glance at some of the foundational
biblical texts – whether the Jewish Old Testament
or the Christian New Testament – to be reminded
of our treacherous roots. According to the Book of
Genesis, Abraham, the first Jew, took his son, Isaac,

to the mountainous region of Moriah, bound him to an altar and then began to wield a knife above his body as a sacrifice to God, until an angel prevented him from doing so. And Jesus, the man who inspired Christianity, died at the hands of a group of murderers who hauled him outside the walls of Jerusalem to Golgotha and then, as described in the Gospel According to Matthew, crucified him, prior to his death from, perhaps, hypovolemic shock or exhaustion asphyxia, resulting in cardiorespiratory failure (Edwards, Gabel, and Hosmer, 1986; Maslen and Mitchell, 2006; cf. Stroud, 1847). Had Abraham lived today, someone would undoubtedly have telephoned social services or the police and would have interrogated him as a potential perpetrator of filicide. In similar vein, the soldiers who crucified Jesus might well have ended up in prison or in a psychiatric institution.

Our ancestors did not hesitate to treat criminals in the cruellest of manners (Du Boys, 1845; Bowen-Rowlands, 1924). Indeed, across the ancient Hebrew, Egyptian, Greek, Roman, and Asian cultures, our predecessors would often inflict sadistic retaliatory punishments upon perpetrators of crime, whether lunatic or not.

12

According to Lewis Lyons (2003), an historian of punishment, human beings have long relied upon four fundamental approaches to the "treatment" of offenders across time, namely: (1) imprisonment; (2) corporal punishment; (3) torture; and, also, (4) capital punishment. Often, perpetrators of violent acts or, indeed, those falsely accused of criminality, would be subjected to all four methods of treatment, each based on punition and retaliation.

During the eighteenth century BCE, the Babylonian king Hammurabi sanctioned an extremely severe code of punishment, which authorised mutilation and amputation of body parts, based on retaliation. According to the recommendations of Hammurabi, if one broke the bone of another person, one would be punished by having one's own bone broken in return; and if one blinded someone else in a fight, one would have one's own eye put out. Similarly, sons who struck their fathers would have their hands severed; rapists would be castrated; and perjurers would have their tongues removed. Burglars would be killed on the spot and then gibbeted (Johns, 1914). Strikingly, these practices of retaliation applied solely to men who injured another person of similar social standing;

therefore, if a wealthy nobleman assaulted and wounded an impecunious servant, he would not receive any punishment for having done so. Women also suffered under Hammurabi's code; indeed, section 129 of the code advised that those accused of adultery should be bound together with their lovers and then thrown into the Euphrates river (Harper, 1904). The code proved so severe that the death penalty could be applied to any infraction ranging from burglary and kidnapping to maintaining a disorderly tavern.

Inspired by Hammurabi, the ancient Greeks punished perpetrators with similar brutality. During the seventh century BCE, Draco, an Athenian lawgiver, came to personify retribution, promoting the death penalty for crimes ranging from murder to the theft of fruit. According to the Greek biographer Lucius Mestrius Plutarch, the cruelty of these laws prompted the orator Demades to describe the pronouncements of Draco as written not with ink but, rather, with blood.[2] The Romans, too, instituted very stiff penalties for criminality, which included not only burning and crucifixion but, also, throwing those convicted of crimes off cliff tops, thus epitomising the *lex talionis* – the law of retaliation (Daube, 1947).

Some unfortunate creatures – often deserters from the army or prisoners of war (Welch, 2007) – would be subjected to *damnatio ad bestias*, namely, being thrown into a public amphitheatre and then torn apart by wild beasts. Chillingly, in his treatise on anger, the Roman statesman and philosopher, Lucius Annaeus Seneca (n.d. [a] [c. 40s CE], p. 97), described this practice as the "beſtiarium immanium caveae", namely, the "pits where monstrous beasts prowl" (Seneca, n.d. [b] [c. 40s CE], p. 20).

According to the Mishneh Torah, the Hebrews would condemn criminals to death through stoning as well as burning, hanging, strangulation, and, also, slaying by the sword (Maimonides, c. 1170 – c. 1180; cf. Johns, 1914; Smith, 1931; Cohn, 1971). And the ancient Chinese practised decapitation at least as early as 2601 BCE and, moreover, endorsed not only execution but, also, branding, mutilation, and castration. During the Zhou dynasty, which began circa 1046 BCE, and, subsequently, throughout the Han dynasty, punishments included cutting off the nose of the offender, branding the forehead, maiming, castration, and death through strangulation or through being sliced to pieces (Alabaster, 1899).

As the centuries progressed, our predecessors perfected innumerable forms of punishment and torture and execution, which would come to include shaming, beating, branding, flogging, confinement to stocks and pillories, ducking in water, imprisonment, breaking on the wheel, mutilation, tearing of the flesh with red-hot pincers, amputation of body parts, not to mention execution through such varied methods as hanging, impalement, stoning, beheading, garrotting, guillotining, boiling, burning, drowning, drawing and quartering, poisoning, shooting with arrows or bullets, starvation and, in more recent years, electrocution or injection of a lethal dosage of drugs (Cawthorne, 2006).

It would be far too simple to dismiss these ancient acts of cruelty as little more than historical excesses perpetrated by the uncivilised brutes of yesteryear. Even the most cultured men and women in recorded Western history have, over the centuries, endorsed such sadistic methods.

For instance, let us recall that Elizabeth, the much-revered sixteenth-century queen who epitomised the so-called "Golden Age" of the English Renaissance, authorised more deaths by official warrant than any other monarch in British history (Childs,

2014). In fact, Elizabeth had no hesitation in employing a full-time torturer, Richard Topcliffe, as a member of her entourage, renowned for his brutal interrogations of prisoners in the Tower of London and for their eventual evisceration (Read, 1925; Richardson, 2004; Hutchinson, 2006). Roman Catholics, in particular, suffered gravely during the reign of Elizabeth. An Englishwoman called Margaret Clitherow, known as the "Pearl of York", had dared to harbour Catholic priests; and, in 1586, although pregnant with her fourth child, authorities condemned her to a particularly vicious death. Stripped of her clothing and forced to lie upon the ground with her hands bound and with a sharp stone positioned under her back, the executioners then placed a wooden door over her torso and subsequently piled "*seven or eight hundred weight at the least*" (Mush, 1849, p. 195) on top of her, which broke her ribs and crushed her to death (cf. Claridge, 1966; Lake and Questier, 2011). This form of torture, known as *peine forte et dure*, would not be legally abolished in Great Britain until the year 1772.

Throughout these earlier centuries, none of the people punished, tortured, or executed, whether truly guilty of their crimes or whether accused unfairly, would have been examined through a psychological lens. We must remember that although madness has existed for thousands of years, the disciplines of psychology, psychiatry, psychotherapy, and psychoanalysis became formalised only in the late nineteenth century; hence, prior to this time, very few, if any, authorities would have considered seriously whether criminals suffered from mental illness, or, in fact, whether early childhood experiences might have contributed to the perpetration of crimes, or, indeed, whether psychological therapy could be offered as an alternative to retribution.

Had Sigmund Freud entered the world several centuries earlier, perhaps he might have consulted to the Tudor queen, Elizabeth, and would have wondered whether the beheading of her mother, Anne Boleyn, authorised during Elizabeth's early childhood by her father, Henry VIII, might have exerted a lingering impact upon the future monarch's subsequent endorsement of executions. By having sanctioned the death of her cousin, Mary of Scotland, in 1587, Elizabeth had thus engaged, quite unconsciously, in an identification with her father. One might argue, therefore, that Elizabeth endeavoured to master the trauma of her own mother's death in 1536 by inflicting precisely the same sentence upon her Scottish cousin almost exactly fifty years later.

Sadly, prior to the twentieth century, even the most well-educated, intellectually sophisticated, and privileged people recommended violent retribution against criminals and, also, those accused of criminality, whether deservedly or undeservedly, whether mad or sane. Alas, most government administrators and clerics in previous centuries lacked any understanding of human psychodynamics and, consequently, the vast majority of law enforcers often projected their own early traumata onto their fragile victims, whom they then tortured and executed as an unconscious means of ridding themselves of any internal memories of their own childhood abuses.

Punishment, torture, and execution have served as mainstays in the treatment of offenders since time immemorial. It would be tempting to argue that no one in the twenty-first century would approve of the *peine forte et dure* – namely, crushing a convicted felon to death. Nowadays, when American states sentence criminals to death, they no longer disembowel or hang them; instead, most convicted felons will die less painfully through lethal injection.

But whether one condemns a felon to death by drawing and quartering, or by hanging, or, indeed, through the arguably less sadistic form of execution by injection, these approaches to the "treatment" of criminality constitute retribution, retaliation, and punishment in the manner of Hammurabi, first devised more than thirty-eight centuries previously. In fact, the allure of treating criminals by torture and, ultimately, by execution has exerted a very powerful attraction throughout the entire canvas of human history. One might argue that the act of murdering those accused of crimes has long appealed to governments, in part, because death as a treatment for dangerous lunatics boasts a 100 per cent success rate. No victim of an execution has ever gone on to commit a further crime!

The grotesque punishment and, often, cruel murder of offenders – whether mad or whether sane – represents perhaps the greatest of human tragedies (e.g., Swain, n.d.). By executing those accused of crimes, our ancestors engaged in an act of unconscious identification with the criminal offence itself, and they, too, became assassins.

With such a long-standing and almost unspeakable history of violence, when did the handling of criminals become less murderous? And when did mental health practitioners first provide a deeper understanding of the causes of dangerous behaviour and a recognition of the fact that many offenders became cruel as a result of early childhood experiences of victimisation?

The medicalisation of insanity:
hereditary taint and the criminal brain

They take refuge in the mad corner of their brain.

(Lady Walburga Paget, *Embassies of Other Days: And Further Recollections. Volume II*, 1923, p. 468)

For centuries, our forebears subjected mad people (including mad criminals) to horrific acts of cruelty and retribution. Even wealthy kings suspected of insanity could be treated in what we would now consider to be a physically abusive manner. For instance, in 1453, the English monarch Henry VI lapsed into a withdrawn catatonic state after the loss of the battle at Castillon, and he became so ill that the Privy Council authorised his royal physicians to bleed him, to shave his head, and to force him to imbibe suppositories and other purgatives (Rymer, 1741; Kahr, 2014b). Mental health professionals per se simply did not exist at that time.

But, during the nineteenth century, the disciplines of psychiatry and criminology began to blossom in parallel, albeit somewhat clunkily. Of course, very few early-nineteenth-century physicians referred to themselves as psychiatrists but, rather, as "alienists", in view of the fact that they assumed responsibility for the so-called "aliens" or mad people whose lunatic behaviours seemed to make little sense. In terms of diagnosis, alienists described their "alien" patients as suffering from either "insanity" or, indeed, from "lunacy", "madness", "mental aberration", "mental alienation", "mental derangement", "mental disorder", a "disordered mind", or, even, from "unsoundness of mind". And as we have already mentioned, those mad people who committed particularly violent crimes would be designated "dangerous lunatics".

In terms of theories of aetiology, these pre-Freudian alienists tended to regard insane people as suffering from an unspecified degenerative brain disease (e.g.,

Colaizzi, 1989). In fact, crime, once considered the work of sinners, became increasingly medicalised. For example, the British alienist Dr. James Cowles Prichard, a Senior Physician at the Bristol Infirmary and, also, a Fellow of the Royal Society, hypothesised that his lunatic patients must have struggled with severe biopathology and, consequently, he would often insist upon post-mortem examinations of those in his care. When, on 8th April, 1819, a black patient from Jamaica called Gard Luke, who hallucinated and who claimed to be the son of God, died from enteritis, Dr. Prichard (1822, p. 314) dissected his body and discovered that the patient had a thick and heavy cranium, ventricles distended with fluid, an inflammation of the abdominal viscera, as well as flabbiness of the right-hand side of his heart, and other abnormalities which could explain the patient's "morbid excitement".

On the basis of the many autopsies performed at his request, James Prichard became convinced that such brain degeneration and other forms of bodily pathology will have contributed to the development of madness, including insanity in those patients who had committed crimes. Prichard (1835, p. 6) established a reputation for having invented the concept of "*Moral*

Insanity", referring to those psychiatrically unwell individuals who lack morality and who, therefore, have no difficulty breaking the law and committing "every species of mischief" (Prichard, 1835, p. 22). Morally insane patients, unlike their ordinarily insane counterparts, often did not hallucinate; but owing to the perversion of their moral compass, these people would perpetrate acts of great cruelty.

Like many physicians during the first half of the nineteenth century, Prichard (1835, p. 184) acknowledged that such factors as domestic grief, disappointment in love, political events, excessive study, alcohol consumption, intestinal disturbances, and, also, "strong passions" could contribute to the development of insanity, but, above all, he trumpeted the role of the degenerate brain. Consequently, he recommended such physical treatments as bleeding, shaving of the head, cold showers or baths with ice, as well as large doses of purgatives such as "tartarised antimony" (Prichard, 1835, p. 267) – a treatment regime no different to the one recommended for the medieval king Henry VI some four centuries previously. Prichard also advised that his lunatic patients should be secluded from society and that they should be whirled round in a special rotatory machine, inducing dizziness and nausea, in the misguided hope of shaking patients, quite literally, out of their lunatic states.

James Cowles Prichard typified the alienist of this period. Most of his colleagues, likewise, regarded insanity as a brain disease best treated by shutting patients away in an asylum, often chained to bed posts or to the walls of their cells (Kraepelin, 1918a, 1918b), or imprisoned in overcrowded gaols. The simplicity of Prichard's work on the degenerative nature of madness – especially moral insanity – eventually spread across the ocean.

Professor Charles Coventry, Professor of Medical Jurisprudence at the Medical Institution of Geneva College, in Geneva, New York, typified the traditional nineteenth-century approach to madness. He argued that, "Probably no case of insanity occurs without more or less derangement of the general health" (Coventry, 1844, p. 143), and that, "the functions of the brain remain impaired" (Coventry, 1844, p. 144). In similar vein, Dr. John Purdue Gray (1857, p. 141), a physician in Utica, New York, concluded that those who perpetrate homicide in mad states of delusion, acute mania, melancholia, sub-acute mania, or dementia, will have done so under the influence of "a marked hereditary predisposition". Indeed, Gray underscored that such patients suffer from either a "*physical disease*" or from some disturbance of health "*in all instances*" (1857, p. 143).

Some physicians argued that one could spot criminals simply on the basis of prominent physical characteristics; for instance, Mr. Bruce Thomson (1870b, p. 332), a Resident Surgeon in Perth, claimed that, "One of the most marked physical characteristics of female prisoners in the General Prison for Scotland is the luxuriant heads of hair which they have." Those women from the so-called "better classes" (Thomson, 1870b, p. 332) sported hair, which Thomson (1870b, p. 332) described, by contrast, as more "silky and fine". Physicians attributed so much importance to these inherited characteristics that most presumed that madness, too, must be embedded in the human body, and that such lunatic qualities can never be altered. In a long-forgotten, but strikingly representative, essay on "The Hereditary Nature of Crime", Thomson (1870a, p. 448) argued that, "the *incurable* nature of crime in the criminal class goes to prove its hereditary nature."

The Italian physician and pioneering criminologist *Professore* Cesare Lombroso greatly expanded upon the work of Prichard; and unlike his fellow Catholics who regarded perpetrators of violent acts as sinners, he, too, endorsed the hypothesis that these men and women suffer from a degenerative disorder of the brain. Based on his study of some 832 delinquents, Lombroso concluded that these criminals possess certain essential physical characteristics. As Lombroso (1876, p. 32) wrote: "In genere, tutti i delinquenti hanno orecchi ad ansa, capelli abbondanti, scarsa la barba, seni frontali spiccati, mento sporgente, zigomi allargati, gesticolazione frequente." ["In general, all the delinquents have ears with handles [jug ears], abundant hair, a poor beard, strong chests, a protruding chin, enlarged cheekbones, and frequent gesticulations."] Over time, Lombroso and his disciples became known as criminal anthropologists, as though they had discovered a rare and faraway species from another land who looked physically different from ordinary human beings.

Through the work of investigators such as James Cowles Prichard and Cesare Lombroso, both insanity and criminality became increasingly medicalised. Few had dared to consider whether early *childhood*

28

experiences might have contributed in any way to the development of madness or violence. Alienists did appreciate that lunacy can often be found among several members of the same family, but these doctors rarely conceptualised intimate domestic experiences and interactions as causative in any way; rather, the preponderance of madness among a group of relatives served merely to confirm the ostensible genetic–biological basis of insanity, which came to be known as "hereditary taint" (Taylor, 1905, p. 819) or as "Triebregungen" (Lange, 1929, p. 89) – a German phrase for innate urges or impulses.

In view of the fact that most nineteenth-century physicians conceptualised mad people – especially *dangerous* mad people – as suffering from brain disease, they offered very little by way of treatment, apart from incarceration and, also, punishment. For instance, in 1872, a seventeen-year-old boy called Arthur O'Connor climbed over the fence into Buckingham Palace and pointed a pistol – albeit unloaded – at the British monarch, Queen Victoria, seated in an open landau alongside her sons, Prince Arthur and Prince Leopold, and her Lady of the Bedchamber, Lady Jane Churchill. The attempted assassination terrified the queen, who later wrote in her journal, "a dreadful thing happened, which God in His mercy averted having any evil consequences" (Victoria, 1872, p. 197). Fortunately, Victoria survived unscathed and the authorities arrested O'Connor. Not long thereafter, the queen's page, Frederick Bruce (1872, p. 200), wrote of O'Connor: "the prisoner was weak-minded and perverse, the easy victim of delusion." Moreover, Bruce (1872, p. 200) described the young lad as suffering from "utter folly, if not insanity". Subsequently, physicians diagnosed him, more formally, as scarred by a hereditary taint; and Baron Anthony Cleasby, the presiding judge, sentenced him to one year's imprisonment as well as twenty strokes from a birch, prior to his eventual committal to an asylum (Geary, 1990).

At that time, the vast majority of specialists recommended incarceration and physical abuse as treatments of choice. But dangerous lunatics could also be sentenced to death. For instance, in 1868, the American courts approved the execution of a woman, Elizabeth Heggie, for having poisoned her two daughters. The aforementioned Dr. John Gray, editor of *The American Journal of Insanity* and a leading psychiatrist of the mid-nineteenth century, described Mrs. Heggie as "cross, irritable, ugly, and repulsive" (Anonymous, 1868, p. 20). Such crude characterisations betoken the lack of compassion of most doctors towards the mad and the dangerous.

In all fairness, some physicians did adopt a more enlightened attitude, such as the British alienist Dr. John Conolly (1856), Consulting Physician to the Middlesex Lunatic Asylum in Hanwell, in the western part of London, who, disgusted by the cruelty of chaining naked patients to their beds, wrote an entire book about the benefits of treating insane men and women without mechanical restraints. On the whole, however, most psychiatric specialists conceived of forensic patients as brain-damaged individuals who should be incarcerated in custodial settings. Few, if any, doctors during the reign of Queen Victoria actually articulated a clear theory of helpful, rehabilitative, or psychologically sensitive forms of treatment.

Indeed, by the second half of the nineteenth century, the cruelty towards psychiatric patients became, arguably, even more chilling, and many patients would be subjected to genital surgery. For instance, women diagnosed as suffering from hysteria would often be hysterectomised, ovariectomised, or even clitoridectomised (e.g., Brown, 1866; Israel, 1880; Church, 1893; Sims, 1893), while insane men, especially those characterised as cases of dementia praecox – the precursor to the modern category of schizophrenia – would have their testicles castrated (Kraepelin, 1913; cf. Kahr, 2018e).

The vast majority of physicians and criminologists of that era provided little insight into the nature of violent crimes. Very few, alas, offered any true compassion or understanding.

Fortunately, a pioneer in Vienna helped to pave the way for a far more enlightened and satisfying approach.

3

The Freudian challenge: towards a humanisation of offenders

seither ist mir die kriminelle Bedeutung
mancher Dinge klar geworden.
[now the criminal significance of some
things has become clear to me.]

(A female patient in treatment with Dr. Sigmund Freud, quoted in a letter from Dr. Sigmund Freud to Dr. Wilhelm Fliess, 28th April, 1897. Quoted in Freud, 1897a, p. 252; Freud, 1897b, p. 238)

In spite of the fact that the vast majority of public officials championed punishment and execution, and in spite of the fact that educated professionals such as physicians and criminologists argued for brain disease as the cause of violence and thus recommended lifelong incarceration, the Enlightenment did, however, spawn some more progressive thinkers who endeavoured to champion the rights and the well-being of violent men and women. For instance, in 1764, Cesare Bonesana di Beccaria, a Milanese aristocrat – son of a *marchese* – published an important tract on crime and punishment, arguing passionately for the abolition of both torture and execution. A visionary of penological reform, Beccaria (1764, p. 138) pleaded, "È meglio prevenire i delitti, che punirli." ["It is better to prevent crimes than to punish them."]

One of Beccaria's contemporaries, John Howard, a Londoner of humble origins who had once worked as an apprentice to a grocer, adopted similarly progressive views. A housing reformer who ultimately became High Sheriff of the county of Bedfordshire, in which capacity he undertook a series of prison inspections, Howard eventually campaigned for more sanitary conditions in prison in order to prevent the spread of disease and, also, lobbied for healthier diets and exercise for inmates. He ultimately testified in the House of Commons about the state of English prisons and published his findings in 1789 (Grünhut, 1941; cf. Howard, 1958; Southwood, 1958; Radzinowicz, 1978).

At the instigation of men such as Beccaria, who

had trained as a lawyer, and Howard, who had become a public servant, prison reform became so increasingly impactful, not only through the efforts of these forward-thinking individuals, but, also, through the championship of novelists. In 1842, after his trip to the United States of America, the Englishman Charles Dickens published his excoriating exposé, not only of the practice of slavery across the Atlantic Ocean but, also, of the horrid state of American prisons, in which the gaolers deprived the prisoners of all contact with the outside world and refused to provide them with any news of their wives or children for years and years. After his visit to a penitentiary on the outskirts of Philadelphia, Pennsylvania, Dickens (1842, p. 238) lamented, "The system here, is rigid, strict, and hopeless solitary confinement. I believe it, in its effects, to be cruel and wrong." After meeting one of the convicts, Dickens (1842, p. 242) described him thus: "He is a man buried alive; to be dug out in the slow round of years; and in the mean time dead to everything but torturing anxieties and horrible despair."

Other literary giants followed suit in their condemnation of such cruelty. In 1862, Victor Hugo produced his masterpiece, *Les Misérables*, which exposed the beastliness of the French penal system, in which the protagonist, "Jean Valjean", had to endure nineteen years of imprisonment for having stolen some bread, simply to feed his family.

By the early 1900s, the growing ideology of libertarian penology – a huge contrast to the more static theories of degenerationism and punishment – even began to penetrate psychiatric institutions. In Sweden, for instance, Professor Olof Kinberg argued for the creation of posts for staff psychiatrists in prisons and recommended that each inmate should be offered a psychiatric examination (Qvarsell, 1993).

But few will have made a more immense contribution to the humanisation of both psychiatry and criminology than the famous Viennese progenitor of psychoanalysis.

Sigmund Freud's work in the field of forensics – the study of public violence and its consequences – began rather inauspiciously. As a young medical student in 1880, Freud undertook his *Rigorosum* examination in forensic medicine, but his examiner, Professor Eduard Hofmann, a distinguished specialist in forensic pathology, failed the would-be physician (Freud, 1900; cf. Jones, 1953). Fortunately, in spite of his early struggles with forensic medicine, Freud became increasingly familiar with the territory when, during his travelling scholarship to France in 1885 and 1886, he attended autopsies at the Paris morgue (Freud, 1886), supervised by the noted physician *Professeur* Paul Brouardel (1897) who, across his career, would examine many cases of death by violence, including instances of infanticide.

Upon his return to Vienna, Freud became increasingly interested in developing new ways of treating the neuroses, having become quite disillusioned by the traditional late-nineteenth-century remedies, which included electrical stimulation of the muscles (e.g., Newth, 1884), hydrotherapy (e.g., Freud, 1886, 1925; cf. Steward, 2012; Large, 2015), and, also, hypnotism (e.g., von Krafft-Ebing, 1895). Through his collaboration with his medical mentor, Dr. Josef Breuer, Freud began to explore the merits of the so-called "talking cure" (quoted in Breuer, 1895, p. 23), and came to appreciate that simply by encouraging free association, patients would have the opportunity to verbalise their hitherto suppressed and repressed sexual and violent thoughts and secrets, and would, as a result, experience a sense of catharsis and relief from neurotic symptomatology. This powerful work provided Freud (1896a, p. 166) with the foundations of the process which he branded, initially in a French neurological journal, as "psycho-analyse", a term which would eventually come to be known, universally, as "psychoanalysis".

Although Freud never worked in an exclusively forensic setting with murderers, rapists, and arsonists, he did encounter numerous destructive individuals throughout his long clinical career; and, in the tradition of Cesare Beccaria, John Howard, and Charles Dickens – his chronological predecessors – he spoke openly about the need to treat violent individuals with greater compassion. For instance, at a meeting of early psychoanalytical disciples on 6th February, 1907, Freud expressed his concern about the cruel punishments inflicted upon offenders. According to Otto Rank, Freud's young colleague who recorded a summary of the discussion, Freud conveyed his sadness at the "unsinnige Behandlung dieser Leute (soweit sie Demenz zeigen) in Gefängnissen" (quoted in Rank, 1907b, p. 101), which translates as the "nonsensical treatment of these people in prisons (in so far as they are demented)" (quoted in Rank, 1907c, p. 108).

Freud knew, by this point, only too well, that every

human being will experience powerful murderous thoughts and feelings. Indeed, as early as 1900, Freud (1900, p. 176) introduced the concept of "Todeswunsch" – "death wish" – into the psychoanalytical literature, thus implying that each of us has the capacity to harbour deadly fantasies. As Freud developed his understanding of the Oedipus complex – the notion that every child struggles with both intensely loving tendencies towards one parent, and hateful, destructive feelings towards the rival parent – he pontificated that murder lies at the very heart of our minds (e.g., Freud, 1912a, 1912b, 1912c, 1913a, 1913b, 1913c).

But Freud did not regard violent, criminal tendencies as a simple, straightforward universal feature of the human being. He came to appreciate that those who suffered from more overtly traumatic or shameful events would be more prone to perpetrate acts of hatred.

For instance, in 1916, Freud wrote about the fifteenth-century English nobleman, Richard, the duke of Gloucester, who subsequently became Richard III for a short period of time. Based on his study of William Shakespeare's magnificent play,[3] written circa 1592, Freud emphasised that Richard's bodily handicaps and infirmities left him "Rudely stampt"

(Act I, Scene i, line 16), so much so, "That dogges barke at me, as I halt by them"[4] (Act I, Scene i, line 23). In particular, Freud emphasised several seminal phrases spoken by Shakespeare's protagonist, which encapsulated the very heart of his murderousness: "And therefore, since I cannot proue a Lover, / To entertaine these faire well spoken dayes, / I am determined to proue a Villaine" (Act I, Scene i, lines 28-30).

Fortunately, Freud did not provide us with merely a simplistic, reductionistic definition of criminality, namely, that trauma results in violence; instead, he offered infinitely greater nuance. Drawing once again on Shakespeare's characters, Freud (1916) noted that the infamous murderess, "Lady Macbeth", the heroine of *The Tragedie of Macbeth*, first performed circa 1606, succumbed to an overt breakdown only *after* she had committed a crime, rather than beforehand, owing to her profound guilt as a successful murderess.

Across the decades, Freud came to anticipate many of the foundational principles of modern forensic psychoanalysis and forensic psychotherapy, namely, the widespread propensity for violent fantasies and, moreover, the potential for those subjected to abuse and trauma to become more likely to enact their hateful thoughts and emotions. Additionally, through his teachings and writings, he expressed not only his regret at the cruel way in which we treat our criminals but, also, his lack of surprise that we should do so. In fact, Freud considered brutal punishment as rather predictable – an unsurprising expression of the ubiquity of human hatred.

In 1931, Sigmund Freud wrote to Professor Georg Fuchs (1931), a German literary critic and political dissident, who had published a book about his own experience of incarceration in a penal institution. Freud (1931b, p. 252) lamented, "I could not subscribe to the assertion that the treatment of convicted prisoners is a disgrace to our civilization. On the contrary, a voice would tell me, it is in perfect harmony with our civilization, a necessary expression of the brutality and lack of understanding which dominate the civilized humanity of the present time."[5] Thus, Freud both condemned cruelty towards offenders while also recognising that punishment serves an important unconscious function among those who have not committed overt crimes.

Sigmund Freud also maintained a long-standing interest in sexual offences against children, having heard direct reports from his adult patients who, during the course of psychoanalysis, spoke of early experiences of molestation (e.g., Freud, 1895, 1896a, 1905; Rank, 1907a). And although he never worked in a prison or in any other overtly forensic setting, Freud certainly came to know about at least two male patients who had abused children sexually. In fact, the father of psychoanalysis conducted the supervision of the treatment of a paedophilic sexual offender, undertaken by his colleague, Dr. Theodor Reik (Natterson, 1966; cf. Kahr, 1991); and he also provided clinical consultations to an Englishman, sent by a British court to Vienna for compulsory psychological treatment, in lieu of a prison sentence (Anonymous, 1995; Kahr, 2010).

On occasion, Freud participated actively in legal proceedings in an effort to assist psychologically vulnerable individuals. For instance, in 1922, Ernst Haberl, son of one of Freud's former servants, shot his father – non-fatally – in an effort to protect his half-sister from sexual molestation. Freud, touched by the plight of this traumatic tale, engaged a lawyer to defend Herr Haberl and even paid for the legal expenses. In fact, the lawyer, Dr. Valentin Teirich, argued that Ernst Haberl suffered from temporary insanity; consequently, the young man did not serve time in prison (Jones, 1957; Aichhorn, 2014).

In addition to his experiences as a forensically sympathetic clinician and as a sometime writer on forensic topics and, also, as a participant in legal cases, Freud cultivated warm relationships with those colleagues who worked more extensively with criminal psychopathology. In 1930, he invited two Spanish-speaking physicians, Professor Nerio Rojas from Buenos Aires and, also, Professor Gregorio Berman from Córdoba – both specialists in forensic medicine – to his home in Vienna (Freud, 1992). He also corresponded with Dr. Grace Pailthorpe, an English physician (Freud, 1933), who had recently produced a report on behalf of the Medical Research Council, arguing for the use of Freudian psychoanalysis in the treatment of violent patients (Pailthorpe, 1932). And he also engaged in a more extended dialogue about criminal psychology with Señor Raúl Carrancá y Trujillo, a Mexican judge who attempted to psychoanalyse offenders, investigating their dreams, their slips of the tongue, and their sexual fantasies (Gallo, 2012).

Freud's compassion towards the violent patient endured across his lifetime. Indeed, when, in 1934, one of his American analysands, Dr. Joseph Wortis – a serious physician in his own right – admitted to certain character failings, Freud replied, sympathetically, "We are not here to judge, not even if you were a criminal" (quoted in Wortis, 1934, p. 55).

Indisputably, Professor Sigmund Freud laid the very foundations for contemporary forensic psychoanalysis by having espoused a sympathetic and non-judgemental attitude towards criminal patients, recognising that every human being harbours a tendency towards violence and that those who have suffered traumata will become much more likely to enact such propensities. Of course, in spite of his recognition of the universality of aggressivity, Freud certainly did not condone violence; and, during later years, he came to know, only too chillingly, about the human capacity for destruction, not least when he had to flee Austria to escape the horror of Nazism. But even so, Freud provided a lens through which subsequent workers could explore the unconscious and infantile roots of crime and might, even, facilitate treatment and rehabilitation (Kahr, 2018c).

The growth of forensic psychotherapy: from punishment to treatment

*Men never commit crimes without
some motive.*

(Dr. James Cowles Prichard, *On the Different Forms of Insanity, in
Relation to Jurisprudence, Designed for the Use of Persons Concerned
in Legal Questions Regarding Unsoundness of Mind*, 1842, p. 126)

Sigmund Freud's writings about human violence certainly inspired a large group of disciples to develop his thinking and its applications; and as early as 1907, Dr. Fritz Wittels, one of the very first Freudian practitioners in Vienna, presented a paper to his colleagues about a Russian woman, Tatjana Leontieva, who had attempted to assassinate a Tsarist official but ended up killing another man instead. Alas, as Wittels had never met this murderess personally, he could offer little more than speculation about the repressed sexual nature of Leontieva's crime (Rank, 1907d). Other early psychoanalysts examined the subject of violence as well. For instance, Dr. Paul Federn (1919), one of Freud's most trusted disciples, produced a tract about the psychology of revolution, in which he dared to wonder whether criminals – especially those who perpetrated acts of violence in order to promote social change – might actually be visionaries. And Alfred Freiherr von Winterstein (1912), another Viennese colleague, argued that, owing to its richness, psycho-analysis must be applied not only within the consulting room but, also, to such diverse fields as art, linguistics, morality, mythology, pedagogy, religion, sociology, and criminology.

During the 1920s, several of Freud's protégés made particularly significant contributions to the study of psychoanalysis and criminality. August Aichhorn, a Viennese schoolteacher of long standing, had spent many years working with delinquent youths. Quite pioneeringly, Aichhorn created a special home in the town of Ober-Hollabrunn for Austrian boys who had committed crimes, which included not only theft but, also, sexual perversions. One of the young patients, for instance, had even worked as a pimp (Mohr, 1966). Having immersed himself increasingly in the psycho-analytical community, Aichhorn became a passionate practitioner who conducted thorough interviews with his delinquent patients and, also, with members of their families. In doing so, Aichhorn (1925, p. 91) succeeded in unearthing the "psychischen Traumen" ["psychical traumas"] which contributed to the development of violent behaviours.

August Aichhorn wrote about heartbreaking cases, including that of the delinquent, vagrant boy whose father died after his twelfth birthday and whose mother – a factory worker – perished violently two years later, mangled in a machine. Aichhorn argued that such profound losses will have contributed to the development of this young person's criminal activities in later years and, moreover, that the acts of delinquency may even have prevented him from plunging into a deep melancholia.

Whereas most experts during the early twentieth century advocated punishment and enforced labour as the appropriate treatment for delinquents, August

Aichhorn (1932) broke new ground. As a forensic pioneer, he offered compassion and, also, psychoanalytical psychotherapy to many of the youthful delinquents with whom he worked.

Psychoanalytical approaches to the study of criminality spread beyond Freud's immediate cluster of colleagues in Vienna to other growing centres of psychological innovation. For instance, in 1913, the Hungarian psychoanalyst, Dr. Sándor Ferenczi, addressed the Reichsverein der Richter und Staatsanwälte [State Society of Judges and Barristers] in Budapest and campaigned passionately for the eradication not only of punishment of offenders but, also, of the abuses perpetrated by prison guards, in favour of psychologically informed treatment. Ferenczi (1919, 1922) campaigned for the development of a psychoanalytical criminology, and he argued that workers must become suspicious of the simple explanations of the causes of violence and that one must elucidate, instead, the deeper, hidden, unconscious origins of crime.

Most impressively of all, the Budapest-born Dr. Franz Alexander, one of Sigmund Freud's protégés and, also, the very first physician to graduate formally from a psychoanalytical institution, made important contributions to the psychological study of crime. Based in Berlin, Alexander (1925) worked with forensic patients at the low-cost Poliklinik für psychoanalytische Behandlung nervöser Krankheiten [Polyclinic for Psycho-Analytical Treatment of Nervous Illnesses], which provided him with extensive clinical experience. Alexander also forged a creative collaboration with Dr. Hugo Staub, a criminologist who subsequently undertook formal training as a psychoanalyst. Together, these two men – great friends to one another (Alexander, 2019) – taught a course about criminal psychology and also co-authored an important book dedicated to the study of "einer psychoanalytischen Kriminologie" (Alexander and Staub, 1929, p. [5]) – "a psycho-analytical criminology" – and, in doing so, drew upon the earlier *cri de coeur* of Sándor Ferenczi.

Based upon the observation that most, if not all, offender patients have little or no insight into why they had perpetrated crimes, Franz Alexander and Hugo Staub argued that investigators must strive to uncover the hidden motivations of violence. They also lambasted the traditional prescription of punishment as "psychologisch unsinnig" (Alexander and Staub, 1929, p. 76), namely, "psychologically nonsensical".

Indeed, these forward-thinking investigators even hypothesised that the prospect of punishment might arouse some of the more masochistic offenders and could, therefore, encourage criminality. Not only did Alexander and Staub critique the biologisation of violence, they also underscored the importance of psychological treatment as a more humane form of intervention. Unsurprisingly, Sigmund Freud (1930) came to regard the work of Alexander and Staub as helpful and as impressive, as did the German judges and criminal lawyers who, eventually, began to welcome a psychological presence in the courtroom (Zilboorg, 1931).

Franz Alexander (1930, 1931a) produced many case histories of psychoanalytical work with dangerous individuals, demonstrating quite cunningly some of the deeper, less obvious aetiological factors which contributed to the development of forensic psychopathology. For instance, in 1931, he published an extraordinary study of a young man who would hire professional chauffeurs to drive him on lengthy journeys in an automobile but who, after each car ride, would then run away without settling his bill. Dr. Alexander (1931b) discovered that, during childhood, this man's stepfather had attempted to chase him out of the family home. With considerable insight, Alexander hypothesised that such a frightening, traumatic experience had impacted greatly and that in an attempt 'to master this trauma, the man developed a criminal habit of running away from father-like chauffeurs, without paying them, so that he could feel in charge of the situation and might thus project his sense of futility and anger into the chauffeurs, whom he cheated on a regular basis.

Through his work as a clinician, as a lecturer, as a writer, and as a physician who testified in court, and through his activities as a researcher who collaborated with a criminologist, Franz Alexander not only helped to lay the foundations for what would, decades hence, become known as forensic psychotherapy or forensic psychoanalysis, but, moreover, he disseminated these novel ideas overseas, beyond the confines of German, Austrian, and Hungarian psychoanalytical circles. During the 1930s, Alexander worked in both Chicago, Illinois and, also, in Boston, Massachusetts, and lectured about psycho-criminological topics (Brown, 1987). He also collaborated with the noted Dr. William Healy – a British-born child psychiatrist and long-time resident of the United States of America – who had already made numerous contributions of his own to the psychological understanding of delinquency (e.g., Healy, 1915; Healy and Bronner, 1922, 1926). Alexander not only psychoanalysed Healy (Gardner, 1972, 1978; Snodgrass, 1984), but, in collaboration, the two men published a groundbreaking book on *Roots of Crime: Psychoanalytic Studies* (Alexander and Healy, 1935).

During his final years, Alexander – then based in Los Angeles, California – continued to lobby for a more humane, psychologically orientated approach to dangerous patients. In collaboration with two fellow Freudian psychoanalysts, namely, the French princess Marie Bonaparte and, also, Dr. Isadore Ziferstein, Alexander petitioned the Governor of California, Edmund Brown, to obtain the release of the convicted robber, kidnapper, and rapist, Caryl Chessman, then incarcerated on Death Row at the California State Prison in San Quentin (Bertin, 1982). Alas, in spite of their efforts, the thirty-eight-year-old Chessman died in the gas chamber.

With powerful contributions from such Central European progenitors as Freud, Ferenczi, Aichhorn, and Alexander, forensic psychoanalysis began to flourish, in small but important ways, all across the globe. In 1925, Dr. Girindrasekhar Bose,[6] the founder of the psychoanalytical movement in India, spoke to the parliament in Calcutta on Freudian theory and its implications for the study of criminality (Anonymous, 1926); moreover, he taught a course about this subject at a special Indian school for detectives (Hartnack, 2001). Bose (1945) would eventually argue that not only might psychoanalysis prove to be a helpful treatment for offenders but, that by intervening early with patients at risk, one might even be able to prevent criminality from developing in the first place. In Argentina, Dr. Juan Ramón Beltrán began to practise Freudian psychoanalytical treatment in a prison setting (Abraham, 1924). And in Melbourne, Australia, Dr. Clara Lazar-Geroe (1942), offered instruction on the psychoanalytical understanding of juvenile delinquency to the local Children's Court Probation Officers.

Although Continental psychoanalysts dominated the growing forensic discourse during the first quarter of the twentieth century (e.g., Merloni, 1933), eventually the British psychoanalysts began to make many vital contributions to the development of this field and have continued to do so to this day. Dr. Maurice Hamblin Smith (1924), an Associate Member of the British Psycho-Analytical Society and, also, a Medical Officer at His Majesty's Prison Winson Green in Birmingham, argued that criminals should be offered proper psychological treatment rather than standard punishment. Likewise, the Vienna-born psychoanalyst, Melanie Klein (1932a), who emigrated permanently to London, and who specialised in the treatment of children, campaigned for early intervention, explaining that children who undergo psychoanalysis will be less likely to become violent offenders in later years.

The Scottish-born Dr. Edward Glover trained as a psychoanalyst in Berlin under the pupillage of Dr. Karl Abraham, Freud's leading German disciple. Upon his return to Great Britain, Edward Glover became a distinguished psychoanalytical practitioner in London and developed an expertise in working with criminal patients. He helped to establish The Association for the Scientific Treatment of Delinquency and Crime, eventually rebranded as The Institute for the Scientific Treatment of Delinquency and, ultimately, as the Institute for the Study and Treatment of Delinquency

(Rumney, 1992), which offered psychotherapy to those who perpetrated acts of criminality. Glover not only enlisted the cooperation of colleagues from the British Psycho-Analytical Society to participate in the running of this new psycho-criminological institution (*Institute Board Meetings: 16.1.1925 to 30.4.1945, 1925-1945*) but, also, he helped to launch a special psychologically orientated periodical, *The British Journal of Delinquency*, and served as its first editor, along with Professor Hermann Mannheim, a noted criminologist, and Dr. Emanuel Miller, an experienced child psychiatrist. Author of numerous publications about sexual perversions and violent crimes (Glover, 1932, 1933, 1936, 1956, 1964) and, also, about the abolition of the death penalty (Glover, 1960, 1961), he devoted much of his professional career to a study of the assessment, diagnosis, and treatment of criminal patients with traditional Freudian methods.

Two of Glover's most brilliant students, Dr. John Bowlby and Dr. Donald Winnicott – also psychoanalysts – developed Glover's forensic foundations in their own very original and very impactful work. Bowlby, one of the founders of the British child psychiatric profession, made an immense contribution when he undertook systematic clinical research on the frequency of early parental loss in the development of subsequent juvenile delinquency. Bowlby (1944a, 1944b, 1945–1946, 1946) will best be remembered for his landmark writings about forty-four juvenile thieves who endured profound separation and loss during their early childhood, which Bowlby came to regard as an important aetiological factor.

In similar vein, Dr. Donald Winnicott, a man who made landmark contributions to many branches of psychoanalysis (Kahr, 1996a, 1996b), devoted a considerable portion of his energies to the study of dangerous children (Winnicott, 1956; cf. Kahr, 2001a, 2001b). Indeed, his very first child analysand – a delinquent boy – certainly vexed Dr. Winnicott (1956) by biting him on the buttocks and, also, by breaking into his automobile and driving it away.

During the ravages of the Second World War, Winnicott served as a psychiatric consultant to children who had to endure evacuation to the countryside; and in this context, he came to appreciate, as did his contemporary Bowlby, that children deprived of regular contact with, and affection from, reliable parental figures will be much more likely to engage in acts of violence. Many of the wartime delinquents with whom Winnicott worked could not be tolerated in ordinary billets and had to be lodged in special residential homes where, in spite of close supervision from staff, they still terrorised the local townspeople and would even set fire to hay ricks (Winnicott and Britton, 1947; cf. Winnicott, 1943, 1945; Winnicott and Britton, 1944). With such wartime knowledge at his disposal, Winnicott (1949) even campaigned to government ministers, urging them to recognise criminality as a form of psychological illness – a rather new idea in the 1940s.

Winnicott best encapsulated his ideas on the early roots of delinquency in a landmark essay, "The Antisocial Tendency", in which he described the case of "John", a young boy who stole from shops compulsively. Although most psychoanalysts in the mid-twentieth century insisted upon working with their patients on a five-times-weekly basis, Winnicott knew that this would not be possible for many families, or, even, necessary; hence, he helped John by talking at length to the boy's mother. With tremendous compassion and insight, Winnicott (1956, p. 307) told the mother, "Why not tell him that you know that when he steals he is not wanting the things that he steals but he is looking for something that he has a right to: that he is making a claim on his mother and father because he feels deprived of their love." The mother did, indeed, follow Winnicott's recommendation; and, rather than simply punishing John as most parents of that era would have done, she engaged the boy in conversation and discovered that he believed that his parents did not love him. Such a frank and touching discussion between a mother and child eventually proved most therapeutic, so much so that, in later years, Winnicott (1968) came to regard juvenile delinquency as a hopeful cry for help.

With John Bowlby (1951a, 1951b) having served as a consultant to the World Health Organization, and with Donald Winnicott (1968) having addressed a Borstal Assistant Governors' Conference and, also, having published in the *Prison Service Journal*, these men succeeded in reaching out to a wide variety of workers in the health care and criminological arenas and thus helped to disseminate depth-psychological knowledge about violent offences. Winnicott also lobbied for the abolition of capital punishment in Great Britain and, on behalf of the Institute of Psycho-Analysis of London, wrote to the Royal Commission on

Capital Punishment, exposing the viciousness of the death penalty and underscoring that the threat of being executed by the state might even entice some people to commit murder (*Memorandum Submitted by the Institute of Psycho-Analysis to the Royal Commission on Capital Punishment,* 1950). Unsurprisingly, Winnicott and his colleagues argued for psychoanalysis as a treatment, in preference to the death penalty.

Having incorporated Sigmund Freud's seminal insights about the importance of early childhood experiences, especially those of a traumatic nature, as well as the utility of the talking cure, the first generations of Freud's disciples made great strides in shaping a field of psychoanalytical criminology. Not only did these pioneering men and women undertake clinical aetiological research and provide assistance to those individuals who committed crimes, they also continued to establish specialist clinics, create periodicals, and consult to government agencies worldwide. For instance, in 1933, the American Psychiatric Association launched a special Section on Forensic Psychiatry under the leadership of Dr. Vernon Branham, a disciple of the influential psychoanalyst Dr. William Alanson White. Branham also became the founding editor of the *Journal of Criminal Psychopathology*, which launched in 1939 (Overholser, 1952), and which holds distinction as the first forensic psychotherapeutic periodical. Other pioneers succeeded in publishing their work in the mainstream medical press rather than in specialist psychoanalytical journals. For instance, Dr. John Charsley Mackwood (1947, 1949), a British medical psychotherapist who worked at His Majesty's Prison Commission, developed psychological work with convicted offenders. Owing to the restriction of resources within the prison service, Mackwood (1949, 1954) championed not only individual psychotherapy but, also, group psychotherapy for criminal patients.

By 1960, the psychodynamic approach to forensic issues had become so much a part of popular cultural discourse that Alfred Hitchcock, the distinguished film director, crowned his masterpiece, *Psycho*, with a scene in which a Freudian-style psychiatrist offers a traditional psychoanalytical explanation of the unconscious motivation of the protagonist, the notorious murderer "Norman Bates". Although this cinematic psychiatrist does not mention the Oedipus complex per se, his encapsulation of Norman Bates's crimes provides strong confirmatory evidence of the way in which Freud's insights had penetrated Hollywood considerably (Farber and Green, 1993).

Although one cannot do justice to the full history of forensic psychotherapy in the space of such a brief communication (Kahr, 2018c), we must single out the work of the noted Argentinian-born, British-based psychiatrist and psychotherapist, *Profesora* Estela Valentina Welldon, who, more than anyone, has expanded and formalised this increasingly important discipline within mental health. Trained by Professor Karl Menninger (1968), one of the greatest of twentieth-century psychiatrists and, also, a passionate critic of punishing the mentally ill, Welldon emigrated to Great Britain and became a long-serving consultant at the Portman Clinic in London – a venerable institution which has provided psychoanalytical psychotherapy for violent perpetrators over many decades. Across her long career, this forward-thinking clinician has made numerous seminal contributions, which include the vital recognition that women, as well as men, have the capacity to commit acts of sexual perversion, notably as abusers of their own bodies and those of their own children (Welldon, 1988, 1991, 1996, 2001, 2011, 2012). Moreover, Welldon (n.d. [1985], 1993, 2011) has drawn upon her training at the Menninger Clinic in Topeka, Kansas, and has helped to pioneer group psychotherapy as a treatment option for forensic patients.

Estela Welldon has distinguished herself not only as a profound forensic clinician but, also, as a most popular teacher and organiser (Kahr, 2018b). She launched a training in forensic psychotherapy – the very first in the world – based at the Portman Clinic and validated by the British Postgraduate Medical Federation of the University of London and by the Faculty of Clinical Science of University College London, also part of the University of London. Moreover, she created the International Association for Forensic Psychotherapy, an organisation which has continued to develop this field in exciting ways.

Drawing upon Welldon's inspiration, the discipline of forensic psychotherapy has continued to flourish. In the United Kingdom alone, the Royal College of Psychiatrists established a Forensic Psychotherapy Special Interest Group; the British Psychoanalytic Council validated the category of "Forensic Psychodynamic Psychotherapist" as suitable for professional registration; and the University of London created the post of Professor of Forensic

Psychotherapy and Medical Education for the distinguished psychiatrist Dr. Gill McGauley who died, sadly, in 2016, shortly after her much-deserved inauguration (Adshead, 2016).

Forensic psychotherapists have made a vital contribution to the understanding of the origins of criminality and to the prevention of violence through early intervention (e.g., Mezey, Vizard, Hawkes, and Austin, 1991; Vizard, Wynick, Hawkes, Woods, and Jenkins, 1996; Vizard, 1997; Kahr, 2004, 2020). By embracing the work of Sigmund Freud and his successors, the current generation of forensic psychotherapeutic mental health professionals has not only treated many violent criminals, but we have also helped to question and to challenge the deeply entrenched notions of offenders as brain-damaged, evil sinners who deserve to be condemned to death. Through the work of pioneers such as Sigmund Freud and Estela Welldon and many others besides, forensic psychoanalytical practitioners have begun to offer a more humane alternative to the understanding and rehabilitation of those who have committed unforgiveable acts of savagery.

5

Paedophilia:
the sexualisation of trauma

Some perverts can, however, be cured by
analysis, and some can only be helped to
sublimate their perverted libido into some-
thing normal and useful.

(Dr. Abraham Arden Brill, *Freud's Contribution to Psychiatry*,
1944, p. 89)

As we know, throughout history, the treatment of dangerous individuals, or even of those suspected of being dangerous, whether "mad" or not, reeks of neglect and cruelty. Fortunately, with the growth of psychoanalytical theory and with the emergence of the new discipline of forensic psychotherapy across the twentieth century, contemporary mental health professionals enjoy many more opportunities to consider compassionate models of treatment and, also, prevention.

Let us now investigate two iconic and chilling categories of forensic psychopathology, namely, paedophilia and murder, and explore not only how our predecessors treated such individuals in the past but, most particularly, the contribution that psychotherapy has made to our understanding of the causes and the cures of such horrific destruction. We shall begin our study by examining the widespread epidemic of sexual offending and, in particular, sexual assaults against children, otherwise known as paedophilia.

Between 2002 and 2007, I served as Principal Investigator of a large-scale study, the British Sexual Fantasy Research Project, examining the erotic thoughts and desires of more than 19,000 adults between the ages of eighteen and ninety-plus. Fortunately, the vast majority of participants in this randomised sample reported sexual pleasure solely from fantasies about fellow adults. But a small number of Britons, approximately one per cent, admitted to masturbatory fantasies about children or, even, infants (Kahr, 2007). In terms of child protection, this statistical data should bring some comfort, knowing that roughly ninety-nine per cent of adults in the United Kingdom prefer grown-ups to children; yet, even one per cent, though quite a small figure, represents, nonetheless, approximately half a million people who often reach climax fantasising about youngsters.

Fortunately, most people who masturbate to the thought of infants or children never enact these fantasies in a concrete physical sense. But, alas, some do possess the capacity to transform their destructive fantasies into painful realities.

I shall never forget that, many years ago, Dr. Brendan MacCarthy, a sometime Consultant Psychiatrist at the Portman Clinic, told me that he had once interviewed a father who had sexually molested his young son on numerous occasions. MacCarthy asked this patient when, precisely, he had first begun to become aroused by his own child, whereupon the man replied, "the moment the doctor in the delivery room announced 'It's a boy!', I had an erection right then and there" (quoted in Kahr, 2016, p. xi).

Sexual crimes against adults and children have plagued human beings for centuries. The ancient Greeks, for example, would frequently perpetrate sexual assaults on small boys and girls (e.g., deMause, 1974, 1988, 1990, 1991, 2002; cf. Kahr, 1991). The practice of older men, in particular, engaging sexually with youngsters became codified as *paiderastia*, namely, the admiration of boys (cf. Langlands, 2006; Davidson, 2007; Orrells, 2015). Indeed, of the numerous ancient Greek amphorae and drinking vessels which have survived, many depict older men touching the genitalia of boys quite explicitly, notably the famous Athenian red-figure ceramic kylix, used for drinking wine, preserved in Oxford's Ashmolean Museum (Lear, 2008).

Tragically, such grisly practices persisted over several thousands of years and often evoked little concern, and, for much of recorded history, those men and women who did molest young children would often be encouraged or ignored. Sometimes, though, offenders would be punished, such as William Dillon Sheppard, a Briton, executed in 1761 for having sodomized a boy (Burg, 2007). At times, even young children themselves suffered physical punishments for having become embroiled in sexual incidents. For instance, in 1624, two eleven-year-old Swiss boys, André Bron and Jean Chaix, accused of having sexual relations with one another and, also, with a four-year-old child, Samuel Moyne, appeared at the court of Geneva, which sentenced them to be beaten in front of their fellow school children (Naphy, 2002). And in 1743, an English boy, molested by an older man, had to endure being pilloried along with his abuser (Burg, 2007).

By the nineteenth century, proof of child rape had become incontestable as the medical literature began to heave with accounts of little children suffering from venereal disease, contracted through sexual intercourse. For instance, Mr. Frederick Lowndes (1887), a surgeon who worked for the Lock Hospital in Liverpool and, also, for the Liverpool Police, encountered numerous cases of girls aged between five and a half and fourteen and a half, subjected to sexual intercourse with older men, some of whom believed, quite falsely, that by molesting a virginal girl they might cure their own pre-existent sexually transmitted diseases (cf. K. J. Taylor, 1985; Bates, 2016). Fortunately, by the nineteenth century, progressive campaigners such as the English investigative journalist William Thomas Stead began to expose the horrors of child prostitution and campaigned to raise the age of consent (Whyte, 1925a, 1925b; Schults, 1972; Ritschel, 2017).

By the third decade of the twentieth century, the

British government finally began to treat the sexual molestation of youngsters with greater seriousness than ever before; and in 1924, Sir Ryland Adkins, a noted judge and former parliamentarian, chaired a Departmental Committee on Sexual Offences Against Young Persons, designed to explore the depth of the problem. The investigation revealed that, over the preceding years, only a very small number of cases of sexual abuse had appeared before the courts of England and Wales. For instance, between 1909 and 1913, a mere forty-three people would be tried for indecent assaults against boys under the age of sixteen and only 593 would be tried for indecent assault against girls under that same age. The authors of the report explained, "there are many more sexual offences committed against young persons than are reported" (Priestley, Fry, Kelly, Martineau, Norris, Parr, Rackham, and Stephenson, 1925, p. 15). Two pioneers of the psychoanalytical movement, Dr. Henry Devine and Dr. Maurice Hamblin Smith, served as witnesses to this committee, thus ensuring the presence of a psychological perspective.

We know that, nowadays, in British courts alone, approximately fifty per cent of all cases involve the

perpetration of sexual offences – many of them paedophilic in nature – resulting in a cash bailout of
£427,000,000 to the Ministry of Justice, simply to fund
the growing administrative workload (Gibb, 2016).

Traditionally, those convicted of paedophilic
assaults would ordinarily be sentenced to prisons or
to long-stay psychiatric institutions and would often
be deprived of any substantial therapeutic interventions. During the 1920s, for instance, it would not be
uncommon for sexual offenders to be imprisoned for
more than fifty years (Cassity, 1927) or, even, executed.
More recently, sexual perpetrators would be dosed
with antipsychotic medications such as benperidol
(Field, 1973), or with antiandrogens such as cyproterone acetate (Davies, 1970; Herrmann and Beach, 1980),
designed to reduce sexual urges (Power and Selwood,
1987), not to mention hormone implants (Field and
Williams, 1970, 1971). Other patients would even be
castrated, either chemically, through the administra-
tion of medications (which could result in softening of
the bones or in enlargement of the breasts) or, indeed,
surgically, through the excision of the testicles (Bremer,
1959; Scott, 1964; Wieser, 1972). Some physicians
even recommended that sexual offenders be subjected

to a hypothalamotomy – a neurosurgical procedure, pioneered by the German neurologist, Professor Fritz Roeder, involving the destruction of the interstitial nucleus of Cajal (Anonymous, 1970; Power, 1976). Other popular treatments deployed in the twentieth century have included electrical aversion therapy and other behavioural interventions (Abel and Osborn, 1996; Dickinson, 2015). But few have explored the potential of depth psychology (and psychoanalysis, in particular) to offer any insight into the nature of sexual offending against young people.

As a fledgling physician, Sigmund Freud (1886) attended demonstrations at the Morgue de Paris conducted by *Professeur* Paul Camille Hippolyte Brouardel (1909), the chair of Médicine Légale [legal medicine] at the Université de Paris; and, as we have already noted, during such visits Freud would have encountered cases of fatal child assault, including those of youngsters who died as a result of rape. One cannot help but wonder whether Freud's (1895, 1896a) exposure to this chilling forensic setting facilitated his subsequent discoveries about the role of early sexually abusive experiences in the life histories of his neurotic patients. Though often lambasted for having underestimated or, even, for having denied the realities of child sexual abuse (e.g., Masson, 1984), Freud encountered cases of sexual cruelty towards young people across his career and readily acknowledged the reality of such traumata. For instance, when supervising the work of his colleague, Dr. Theodor Reik, who had begun to psychoanalyse a sexual offender, Freud remarked, "He must have been seduced as a child" (quoted in Natterson, 1966, p. 256).

Quite pioneeringly, Freud not only encountered adult perpetrators of sexual violence towards children (e.g., Freud, 1905; Anonymous, 1995; Kahr, 2010), but he came to appreciate that young siblings could also harm one another, often in the wake of a previous assault perpetrated by an adult. For instance, as early as 1896, Freud (1896b, p. 152) observed:

> In seven out of the thirteen cases the intercourse was between children on both sides – sexual relations between a little girl and a boy a little older (most often her brother) who had himself been the victim of an earlier seduction. These relations sometimes continued for years, until the little guilty parties reached puberty; the

boy would repeat the same practices
with the little girl over and over again
and without alteration – practices to
which he himself had been subjected by
some female servant or governess and
which on account of their origin were
often of a disgusting sort. In a few cases
there was a combination of an assault and
relations between children or a repetition
of a brutal abuse.[7]

Inspired by Freud's suspicion that early psychological traumata might well contribute to the development
of sexual crimes in later life, several pioneering psychoanalytical practitioners began to expand upon his work
(e.g., Happel, 1925). For instance, Dr. John Holland
Cassity (1927) – an early member of the American
Psychoanalytic Association – underscored the role of
traumatic weaning experiences during the infancy of
sexual perpetrators, which, he argued, might stir aggressive tendencies in later life. One of Cassity's patients
in the criminal department at St. Elizabeths Hospital
in Washington, D.C. – a fifty-two-year-old male – had
molested a seven-year-old girl. Through his psycholog-

ical investigations of this patient, Dr. Cassity uncovered important biographical information. First, he learned that, during breastfeeding, the mother used to apply charcoal to her nipples in a desperate attempt to wean her baby son. One can only wonder whether this might have contributed to the patient's ultimate loathing of the adult female, preferring the unsullied body of a young girl with no repellent charcoal on her chest. Second, Cassity learned that his future patient, during youth, would masturbate with domestic animals – by no means a normal expression of the child's libidinal urges and, as we now realise, an early warning sign of the development of sexual perversion in later life.

In this landmark study, John Cassity had under-scored the role of early trauma in the development of paedophilia. Moreover, he recognised the urgent need to address the treatment of this type of psychopathol-ogy, not least as one of his institutionalised patients had engaged in sexual relations with no fewer than fifty young girls prior to his eighteenth birthday.

Dr. Ben Karpman (1950), another American forensic psychiatrist deeply immersed in psychoana-lytical ideas, reported a case of a paedophile who, as a youngster, became frightened by the sight of female genitalia and developed an attraction to the bodies of children instead, which seemed far less threatening. Karpman's insights, like those of Cassity before him, helped to underscore that a fear of the adult female body might serve as a contributory factor in the development of a paedophilic state of mind.

In 1955, Dr. Emanuel Hammer, a psychoanalytically orientated psychologist, and Dr. Bernard Glueck, Jr., a psychoanalyst and psychiatrist, published a very revealing study of over 200 sexual offenders incarcerated in the Sing Sing Prison in the village of Ossining, New York. The authors observed that these sexually abusive patients – especially those accused of paedophilia – suffered from a fear of heterosexual contact with adult females and that many experienced a deep sense of genital inadequacy. When these paedophilic perpetrators responded to the Rorschach ink blots – undoubtedly the most popular and most long-standing of projective tests – approximately ninety per cent reported seeing such images as a dog with a mutilated tail, or a withered human finger, or a one-legged man – all indicative of marked castration anxiety. Thus, Hammer and Glueck (1955) conceptualised adult paedophilia as a response to the internal sense of genital insufficiency and as a consequent struggle to feel potent with a fellow adult.

In similar vein, Dr. Manfred Guttmacher, a psychoanalytically sympathetic psychiatrist, and Professor Henry Weihofen, a lawyer, published a case report about a shy twenty-year-old man called "Charles" who attempted to rape a five-year-old girl. The authors noted that Charles possessed an undescended testicle, which challenged his sense of masculine potency; furthermore, his mother had warned him about the dangers of sexual relations with adult females. Unsurprisingly, Charles harboured a great fear of becoming genitally impotent. Having encountered many such patients with similar anxieties, Guttmacher and Weihofen (1952, p. 115) described sexual offenders as "insecure" adults and, hence, more likely to attempt contact with children.

These proto-Freudian conceptualisations might seem somewhat anecdotal, or even flimsy, to contemporary health care practitioners who now work in a more highly technologised era of blood tests and brain scans. Nevertheless, these early psychoanalytically inspired case reports, based on detailed conversational studies of sex offenders, serve as a powerful reminder that many of the men who committed such crimes had reported impactful experiences in their own lives which, they believed, had contributed to the development of their subsequent state of mind.

In 1959, Dr. Charles Socarides, a psychiatrist and psychoanalyst based in New York City, authored the first truly comprehensive paper on the Freudian understanding of sexual offences against children, the landmark "Meaning and Content of a Pedophiliac Perversion", published in the *Journal of the American Psychoanalytic Association*. In this essay, Socarides described a male paedophile patient in his late thirties who had suffered considerable mistreatment during his own childhood. As a young boy, this future offender often went hungry and, also, witnessed his father treating his mother in a manner both "cruel and vicious" (Socarides, 1959, p. 87). At the age of five years, the boy's mother despatched him to an orphanage, promising to return for him the next day. Alas, she never did so, and, in consequence, this future paedophile became terrified. By the age of eight years, he experienced visual hallucinations of a menacing Jesus Christ. From his eleventh year, this boy began to hold his breath – perhaps as an unconscious (or even conscious) attempt to commit suicide. And during his twelfth year, some of the other boys in the orphanage began to perform fellatio and masturbation upon him, as did an adult member of staff.

As this youngster approached puberty, he dreaded the onset of secondary sexual characteristics, which evoked fears of ageing and death. In order to ward off such anxieties, Socarides's future patient began to engage in sexually abusive assaults on younger boys; and from at least the age of eighteen he would ejaculate intracrurally, between the thighs of his chosen victims. He particularly enjoyed attacking pampered boys who had grown up in good homes and who had experienced much parental love. Not only did such paedophilic episodes constitute an envious attack but, also, a profound wish to incorporate the goodness of the boys which this young man craved for himself.

According to Socarides, this paedophile would indulge his own wish to *be* a boy; and during the sexual assaults, he would fuse with the boy in his mind, fantasising the two bodies as one. The patient exclaimed, "I have to think I'm a part of him or he's a part of me. I can only have an ejaculation if I imagine we're together, we are *merged*. Almost like two pictures coming together. I'm on top of the child and the feeling is that

I'm a part of him" (quoted in Socarides, 1959, p. 89).

Socarides's 1959 case report, rarely cited in the broader psychological literature, provides compelling evidence not only of the structure of the patient's unconscious mind but, also, of the traumatic background so characteristic of the future paedophilic perpetrator. Moreover, Socarides offered psychoanalytical treatment to this patient and, happily, as a result of this sustained piece of clinical work, the paedophilic perversion remitted successfully.

Nearly thirty years after the publication of this groundbreaking essay, Charles Socarides (1988) produced an expanded version of the case history in which he revealed that his patient suffered, unsurprisingly, from extreme self-loathing and that he regarded human beings – himself included – as little more than cockroaches. As the patient revealed to his psychoanalyst, "Man is a pimple. He is rotten and he is worthless. He has done nothing to change the world and he never will" (quoted in Socarides, 1988, p. 467). Thus, Socarides has helped us to appreciate not only the potential for psychoanalytical treatment to expose the traumatic origins of paedophilia but, also, to obtain a deeper understanding of the self-hatred which the sexual offender projects into the helpless victim.

Charles Socarides (1991) persevered in his study of paedophilia across his long career and, after decades of further clinical research, he published a short, but rich, essay on "Adult–Child Sexual Pairs: Psychoanalytic Findings", in which he identified no fewer than eleven hallmark characteristics of long-standing invariant paedophile patients. According to Socarides, career paedophiles suffer from the following symptoms or mental states:

1. A splitting of the ego.
2. A high degree of paranoid symptomatology and a fear of engulfment.
3. The use of splitting as a mechanism of defence.
4. A fear of punishment and a guilt-laden superego.
5. A history of child sexual abuse and an early onset of the offending behaviours.
6. A family background often consisting of cruel mothers and uncaring fathers, with a high incidence of early childhood injuries and other traumatic events.

7. A history of separation traumas, which might include hospitalisations, surgical operations, or changes of residence.
8. A marked fear of disintegration of bodily boundaries.
9. A primary feminine identification (among male perpetrators) with the mother's body.
10. A tendency for the paedophilic perpetrator to identify with the child victim, thus permitting the perpetrator to incorporate the youthfulness of the child and recreate the mother–child relationship unconsciously.
11. A high degree of death anxiety.

Socarides argued that paedophiles who assault children of the same gender do so in order to feel more potent. He noted that, "the major mechanism in homosexual pedophilia was incorporation of male children in order to reinforce the sense of masculinity, overcome death anxiety and remain young forever, as well as return to the maternal breast" (Socarides, 1991, p. 189). Thus, deprivation, abuse, and family violence will often contribute to the development of paedophilia during later life and will prompt the male sexual offender to attack young boys or girls in an attempt to destroy their beauty and innocence and, also, to recapture his own lost childhood through these cruel and perverse assaults.

Across the Atlantic Ocean, a number of British psychoanalytical mental health professionals also began to tackle the problem of paedophilia, in particular, the South African-born, London-based Dr. Mervin Glasser, who worked for many years at the aforementioned Portman Clinic, a specialist facility that has, for decades, offered dynamic psychotherapy to offender patients. Glasser (1988), like Socarides, endeavoured to provide psychoanalytical treatment for paedophiles, underscoring that although one cannot condone such criminal offences, one can, nevertheless, provide psychological help instead of, or in addition to, restraint.

On the basis of his many years of clinical experience in a forensic psychotherapeutic institution, Glasser came to differentiate between "*Primary paedophilia*" and "*Secondary paedophilia*" (1988, p. 122). Those suffering from primary paedophilia (such as Charles Socarides's aforementioned patient) have struggled with a long-standing preoccupation with children over many years and have invested a great deal of time and energy into the grooming and assault of young boys and girls. Those diagnosed with secondary paedophilia, by contrast, will often attack children as a consequence of other mental health conditions such as schizophrenia, the organic psychoses, or disintegrated personality disorders. Both the primary paedophile and the secondary paedophile inflict immense harm on children.

Glasser (1988, p. 122) studied primary paedophilia, in particular, in great detail, and he noted that one can divide this category further into "*Invariant*" paedophilia and "*Pseudoneurotic*" paedophilia. The invariant male paedophile – often drawn to boys rather than girls as targets – will lead a very lonely, barren existence, characterised by a deep obsession with children or adolescents. Many invariant paedophiles will be burdened by intellectual disabilities or other forms of handicap and thus feel unable to compete in the world of mature, adult relatedness. Pseudoneurotic paedophiles, by contrast, will often have the capacity to engage in adult heterosexual contact (unlike the invariant paedophiles), but many will have enjoyed fantasies of sexual intercourse with young children while sleeping with adult partners. During stressful periods, the pseudoneurotic paedophile will regress and will engage in sexual contact with children, rather than with adults. Needless to say, Glasser regarded both the invariant paedophile and the pseudoneurotic paedophile as cases of severe sexual perversion.

Throughout his work at the Portman Clinic, Mervin Glasser came to appreciate that most men who engage in criminal sexual activity struggle to maintain intimate adult relationships and will often invest their erotic energies into the violation of children as a way of experiencing sexuality without having to endure the burdens of prolonged intimacy. Glasser (1979, p. 278) referred to this state of mind as the "*core* complex" – the ultimate psychopathological expression of an approach-avoidance style of relatedness.

Over time, Glasser's work with adult, male paedophiles has become increasingly influential in the United Kingdom, especially within the broader psychoanalytical community, and it continues to be cited in essays and bibliographies (e.g., Hopper, 1991, 1995; Hakeem, 2009). But Glasser's clear and illuminating descriptions of the paedophilic mind have garnered respect even from those not steeped in Freudian thought. Indeed, two distinguished non-psychoanalytical psychiatrists, Professor Robert Bluglass and Dr. Paul Bowden, invited Glasser (1990) to contribute a chapter on paedophilia to their large textbook on *Principles and Practice of Forensic Psychiatry* (Bluglass and Bowden, 1990). Glasser proved sufficiently adept at working psychotherapeutically with practising paedophiles that, even after his death in 2000, reports have continued to appear in print by former patients who have thanked him publicly for having helped to facilitate a cure (e.g., Dawson, 2016).

Although many people assume that most, if not all, sexual crimes against young people will inevitably be committed by adult *males*, forensic psychotherapists have questioned this stereotype and have reported on the widespread occurrence of paedophilic crimes perpetrated by adult *females*. More than any other worker in this field, *Profesora* Estela Welldon (1988), author of a paradigm-shifting book, *Mother, Madonna, Whore: The Idealization and Denigration of Motherhood*, has alerted us to the potentiality of women to harm not only their own bodies but, also, those of their children. In her seminal book, and in her other insightful writings, Welldon (1991, 1996, 2001, 2011, 2012) has made a huge contribution to our understanding of the nature of sexual crimes against youngsters (cf. Motz, 2008, 2009; Adshead, 2018).

And, perhaps most shockingly of all, not only do adult men and adult women harm young children in a sexual manner, but so, too, do other *children*; indeed, a very significant percentage of sexual crimes against babies and youngsters will be perpetrated by other children or adolescents (National Children's Home, 1992; cf. Hurry, 1990; Campbell, 1994; Lanyado, Hodges, Bentovim, Andreou, and Williams, 1995). More than a century ago, Sigmund Freud (1896a, 1896c) had commented upon the frequency of sexual relations between siblings during childhood; and in the decades that followed, several of his disciples worked with young people who harmed other boys and girls in a sexual manner. For instance, Dr. Melitta Sperling (1978), a noted American psychoanalyst who specialised in the treatment of psychosomatic disorders in children, presented several cases of sexually deviant youngsters. To cite but one example, Sperling (1959) reported on the case of "Rhoda", a six-and-a-half-year-old girl who would bribe her classmates with sweets and would then inspect their genitals in the school toilet, with her own underpants pulled down. Rhoda would also hit other girls upon their naked bodies, demonstrating the close admixture of eroticism and sadism. Dr. Sperling discovered that, as a child, Rhoda had witnessed her mother and her grandmother engaged in physical fights during which neither wore any clothing!

In 1992, a British forensic child psychiatrist and psychoanalyst, Dr. Eileen Vizard, established the Young Abusers Project, a programme co-sponsored in its early days by the Tavistock Clinic of London, in association with the National Children's Home, the National Society for the Prevention of Cruelty to Children and, also, the United Kingdom's Department of Health, designed to provide psychoanalytically orientated assessment and psychotherapy for young child and adolescent sexual offenders in the hope of forestalling any future sexual attacks. This visionary project made an important contribution to the understanding of child sex abusers, many of whom had already committed serious offences against younger boys and girls, having demonstrated inappropriate, sexualised behaviours at home or in school. Vizard and her colleagues identified not only young boy perpetrators but, also, young girl perpetrators for whom the team would provide in-depth assessments of risk before advising on psychotherapeutic treatment options (e.g., Vizard, Monck, and Misch, 1995; Vizard, Wynick, Hawkes, Woods, and Jenkins, 1996; Vizard, 1997; Woods, 1997; Kahr, 2004, 2020).

During the 1990s, I had the privilege of serving as a member of the Young Abusers Project clinical team, providing ongoing psychoanalytically orientated psychotherapy to quite a number of the patients, all of whom had raped children far younger than themselves. To my great surprise, every single one of the adolescent boys with whom I worked engaged in what I have come to refer to as "leg-splaying behaviour". After entering my consulting room and seating themselves in a chair, these young sex offenders would spread their legs as widely as possible, underscoring that they could communicate only with their genital region, rather than with words – such a contrast to other male psychotherapy patients who keep their legs closed tight. One of these teenage boys, who had raped several very young girls, would often place his large, bulky mobile telephone (long before the days of the slimmer iPhones) between his two openly spread legs, so that the telephone would resemble a symbolic penis. As one uses a telephone primarily for the purpose of speaking, this patient managed to concretise in rather a dramatic fashion exactly how he would talk only with his genitals.

Forensic psychotherapists endeavour to rectify the situation by helping our patients to communicate with their voices rather than with their sexual organs. Fortunately, through this sustained and detailed psychotherapeutic work, my colleagues and I made significant headway in facilitating these young offenders to work through their rage and thus cease their violent activities (Kahr, 2020).

As a result of Eileen Vizard's visionary work, she received one of the most prestigious of Royal decorations and became a Commander of the Most Excellent Order of the British Empire (CBE). I cannot do justice to the contributions of Vizard and her colleagues at the Young Abusers Project in such a brief context, but I certainly came to appreciate that psychotherapy does, in fact, reduce the likelihood of reoffending quite considerably, especially after the young patients have had an opportunity to verbalise their early traumatic experiences and to obtain both catharsis and insight (Kahr, 2004, 2020).

Unquestionably, paedophilia represents one of the greatest threats to the safety of children's bodies and children's minds; and we now know, only too chillingly, of the devastating consequences for boys and girls who have suffered abuse. Therefore, every mental health worker has an obligation to recognise the warning signs of harmful sexual activities among both potential victims and, moreover, potential perpetrators. In this respect, the psychoanalytical research on the role of traumatisation in the origin of sexual offending remains of primary importance.

Needless to say, many people insist that even if paedophiles – whether adult male perpetrators, female perpetrators, or child perpetrators – have suffered great abuse themselves during their formative years (e.g., Hackett, Masson, Balfe, and Phillips, 2013), this does not excuse their behaviour. I agree entirely. Many have argued that, in view of the violence of paedophilic behaviour, only chemical castration or surgical castration or lifelong incarceration will suffice, and some have, of course, questioned the desirability of offering psychotherapy at all, which many have construed as far too soft an option (cf. Adshead and Mezey, 1993). Of course, most psychoanalytical practitioners would agree that many long-standing, invariant paedophiles should be treated only in an institutional setting, and there may be much merit in this argument. After all, potential child victims must be kept physically safe, first and foremost.

But the investigations undertaken by generations of psychoanalysts, and my own clinical experience as well, have led me to recognise that psychotherapy provides a very effective remedy for paedophilic patients, especially after one helps the patient to obtain insight into the impact of his or her deeply traumatic history. Certainly, whatever one comes to think about the advisability of offering the talking cure for dangerous paedophilic lunatics, mental health workers agree that every single paedophile will invariably have experienced gross abuses during the early years of development. Not a single colleague has ever identified a paedophile who had enjoyed a happy, trauma-free childhood. Therefore, we must all endeavour to do what we can to prevent child abuse in the home and in schools; and by doing so, we will reduce the likelihood of future paedophiles haunting our streets.

Murder:
the castration of safety

*Crimes against persons are not always as
easy to classify and understand as crimes
against property. These acts are so numerous
and come from so many different emotions
and motives, that often the cause is obscure
and the explanation not easy to find.*

(Clarence Darrow, *Crime: Its Cause and Treatment*, 1922, p. 81)

Nothing causes more distress and heartbreak than
murder. Indeed, in 1869, William Edward Hartpole
Lecky (1869, p. 46), the noted Irish historian, encapsulated the devastation of this most cruel of crimes,
arguing that, "every instance of murder weakens the
sanctity of life." Few would disagree.

But what actually prompts someone to commit the irreversible act of murder? Does killing result from pure evil or from insanity?

While our ancient predecessors regarded murder as a punishment inflicted by the gods, and our medieval forebears considered killing as the work of the Devil, by the nineteenth century physicians came to conceptualise murder as proof of brain disease. For instance, in 1869, an American, Daniel McFarland – a drunkard whose unfaithful wife had just divorced him – shot his sexual rival with a pistol. The victim died some days later in the arms of McFarland's former spouse. Dr. William Hammond and Dr. Reuben Vance, two of the psychiatrists who testified in this case, diagnosed congestion of the brain as the probable cause of McFarland's brutal homicide (Clouston, 1870; Anonymous, 1871; cf. Cooper, 1994).

Psychiatric specialists had little difficulty pontificating about the putative neurological causes of murder. But in terms of treatment, most physicians failed to provide adequate remedies beyond institutionalisation. For instance, in 1845, Dr. Samuel Woodward (1845, p. 325), Superintendent of the State Lunatic Hospital in Worcester, Massachusetts, offered a consultation to a twenty-five-year-old man, known as "G.E.", who revealed the depth of his murderous wishes and his fear that he might kill quite a number of people. Dr. Woodward provided merely some unspecified dietary recommendations and encouraged G.E. to return for another appointment if the murderous impulses did not abate. Roughly two months later, Woodward (1845, p. 326) wrote, "Not having heard from him since, I hope that the dreadful impulse has again passed from his mind." This case typifies the relative neglect of those at high risk of perpetrating such a dangerous crime.

Likewise, in 1863, in the middle of the American Civil War, a fifty-four-year-old physician from Norfolk, Virginia, Dr. David Minton Wright, shot and killed a soldier, Lieutenant Alanson Sanborn. In the wake of this murder, the President of the United States of America, Abraham Lincoln (1863), invited the afore-mentioned Dr. John Gray of the New York State Lunatic Asylum to perform an independent examination of the assassin. Gray found "nothing particular in his early history" (Anonymous, 1864, p. 290) which might be of concern.

Although John Gray, the alienist, offered little

insight into the cause of Dr. David Minton Wright's murder of an American soldier, we know that, not long before the killing, Dr. Wright's son had fought in the Battle of Gettysburg, in Pennsylvania – a brutal military encounter which resulted in the death or injury or capture of tens of thousands of soldiers (Burrage, 1906; Patterson, 1997; Guelzo, 2013). Dr. Wright, alas, did not know whether his son had survived the battle or whether he had perished; consequently, he became "incoherent" (quoted in Anonymous, 1864, p. 296) and, thus, at great risk of breakdown. Arguably, one might hypothesise that Dr. Wright became inconsolable at the prospect of the death of his own child, but the authorities simply branded him as insane and eventually hanged him.

The aforementioned cases of two convicted killers, Daniel McFarland and David Minton Wright, and that of a potential killer, G.E., typify the nineteenth-century approach to both the biologisation and the neglect of serious criminality. But while psychiatrists dismissed murderers as suffering from congestion or degeneration of the brain, a small number of more forward-thinking physicians did, however, endeavour to identify the potential aetiological role of environmental factors. Singularly, Dr. Isaac Ray (1866), one of the founders of American psychiatry, published an important essay in *The American Journal of Insanity* about two women who killed their sometime lovers in the wake of painful romantic rejections or assaults, thus suggesting that not every murderer commits a crime coincidentally.

Alas, since the nineteenth century, traditional psychiatrists have made very few strides in the understanding of the causes of murder. In 1986, Professor John Gunn, Professor of Forensic Psychiatry at the Institute of Psychiatry of the University of London and, for many years, one of the most distinguished practitioners in the United Kingdom, expressed his uncertainty about the causes of murder when commenting upon such serial killers as Peter Sutcliffe, better known as the "Yorkshire Ripper", and Kenneth Erskine, the "Stockwell Strangler". As Professor Gunn lamented, "Apart from the fact that they are all suffering from some form of mental disturbance, there is unfortunately no common thread" (quoted in Berlins, 1986, p. 10). Professor Gunn's protégé, Dr. Pamela Taylor (1985, p. 495) – subsequently a Professor in her own right – argued that violent offences can often be

"Motiveless" and that "Motives are elusive" (P. J. Taylor, 1985, p. 491), explaining that crimes often result from mental illness, rather than from the traumata which might underpin the mental illness in the first place.

Desperate for an explanation of such horrific human behaviour, twentieth-century investigators, like their nineteenth-century forebears, championed biological explanations of extremely violent behaviour. Dr. Edward Podolsky (1956, p. 43), an American psychiatrist, described murder as a "bizarre" crime and one that often seems "motiveless" (p. 44), but which, in fact, can be explained by such physiological abnormalities as hypocalcaemia – low levels of calcium in the blood serum – a condition that often results in extremes of motor activity.

In 1964, a team of physiologists at the National Institute for Medical Research in London discovered that, by implanting electrodes into the brain stems of cats, they could exacerbate a startle reaction and hence increase the potential for vicious attacks, thus implying that the roots of cruelty might be of electro-physiological origin (Abrahams, Hilton, and Zbrożyna, 1964). Likewise, other investigators, such as Professor James McBride Dabbs, Jr., a social psychologist and behavioural endocrinologist at Georgia State University in Atlanta, Georgia, discovered that those prisoners with higher concentrations of salivary testosterone will be more likely to have perpetrated acts of extreme violence, such as rape, child sexual assault, and homicide (Dabbs, Frady, Carr, and Besch, 1987; Dabbs and Dabbs, 2000; cf. Brooks and Reddon, 1996). And several neuropsychological researchers, such as Professor Charles Golden of Nova Southern University in Fort Lauderdale, Florida, have suggested that violence might result from prefrontal brain damage and temporal lobe dysfunction (e.g., Golden, Jackson, Peterson-Rohne, and Gontkovsky, 1996). Others, such as Professor James Fallon (2013, p. 74), an American neuroscientist, have even argued for the presence of a so-called "warrior gene".

Perhaps, most influentially of all, Professor Adrian Raine, a British-born psychologist and neurocriminologist, based previously at the University of Southern California in Los Angeles, California, and currently at the University of Pennsylvania, in Philadelphia, Pennsylvania, has obtained positron emission tomography scans and, also, magnetic resonance imaging scans of the brains of murderers. His investigations have revealed a range of abnormalities, including a decreased glucose metabolism in the lateral prefrontal cortex and medial prefrontal cortex (Raine, Buchsbaum, Stanley, Lottenberg, Abel, and Stoddard, 1994), as well as asymmetries in the amygdala, thalamus, and medial temporal lobe (Raine, Buchsbaum, and LaCasse, 1997). Raine and colleagues also discovered that those men diagnosed as suffering from antisocial personality disorder would be much more likely to reveal a reduction in the volume of grey matter in the prefrontal cortex (Raine, Lencz, Bihrle, LaCasse, and Colletti, 2000), as well as a bilateral reduction in the volume of the amygdala (Yang, Raine, Narr, Colletti, and Toga, 2009; cf. Raine, 2013).

Needless to say, many biomedical researchers have attempted to discover neurological contributory factors in the genesis of severe violence. For instance, the American neuropsychologist Professor Jordan Grafman, in collaboration with his team at the Veterans Head Injury Program of the Uniformed Services University of the Health Sciences in Bethesda, Maryland, discovered that those head-injured veterans with lesions in the ventromedial prefrontal lobe would be at increased risk of verbal, but not physical, aggression (e.g., Grafman, Schwab, Warden, Pridgen, Brown, and Salazar, 1996; cf. Grafman, Schwab, Pridgen, and Salazar, 1995). Nevertheless, it remains uncertain, however, whether researchers have demonstrated that biomedical factors, either genetic or neuropathological, have played a truly causal role in the perpetration of crime. As Professor Joseph Alper (1995, p. 273), a distinguished American chemist and geneticist, has argued, investigations which have trumpeted the so-called biological causes of crime may be "far too preliminary".

The aforementioned researchers have prioritised the study of potential biological vulnerabilities which might, or might not, contribute to the development of murderousness. In a more nuanced fashion, Professor Jonathan Pincus (2001), a neurologist at the Georgetown University Medical Center, in Washington, D.C., identified brain abnormalities in several of the murderers whom he had examined. But, although sympathetic to the impact of neuropathology, Pincus also collaborated with Professor Dorothy Otnow Lewis, a forensic psychiatrist at the New York University School of Medicine in Manhattan, who, on the basis of her research, discovered that the vast majority of murderers had either witnessed or experienced violence during childhood, thus predisposing them to considerable hatred in later life. In one of her early studies, Lewis and her team discovered that, in a sample of thirty-seven young people condemned to death in the United States of America, at least twelve had survived acts of physical brutality and at least five had endured being sodomised by relatives (Lewis, Pincus, Bard, Richardson, Prichep, Feldman, and Yeager, 1988). And in a subsequent study, Lewis and colleagues obtained independent corroboration that eleven out of the twelve murderers in their research sample had suffered severe abuse (Lewis, Yeager, Swica, Pincus, and Lewis, 1997; cf. Lewis, 1998).

Twentieth-century investigators have undertaken far more sophisticated neurobiological research than their predecessors, and it may well prove to be the case that many individuals who commit murder might reveal such biomarkers as heightened levels of testosterone or abnormalities of the prefrontal cortex. However, much neurocriminological work poses considerable problems, first and foremost the fact that not every person with such biomarkers will commit murder and, moreover, not every person who engages in murder will display these biological abnormalities. Moreover, whether a murderer does suffer from the weight of these biopathological irregularities, we must consider the role that early childhood trauma might play in the genesis of murder. Virtually every single forensic patient with whom my colleagues and I have worked has suffered from a dreadful early life history, full of physical violence, parental rejection, and sexual abuse. What impact do such psychogenic pathogens have upon the development of killers? Very few investigators have dared to consider whether real-life traumata might well be the common thread in cases of murder.

Whereas nineteenth-century asylum physicians have claimed that murder results from degeneration of the brain and, in similar vein, twentieth-century researchers have emphasised the role of more specific neurological and biochemical pathologies, modern psychoanalysts, by contrast, have underscored the role of intrapsychic and intrafamilial factors in the traumatic histories of men, women, and children who kill. Indeed, as we indicated in Chapter 3, Freud had observed that every human being has the capacity to experience a "Todeswunsch" – a death wish – especially towards parents, siblings, spouses, and children. For Freud, the urge to kill constitutes a normal underbelly of human fantasy.

Fortunately, most of us will never, ever enact our murderous fantasies and wishes. What factors, then, beyond heightened levels of testosterone and other biological markers, might contribute to the perpetration of the ultimate crime?

Without doubt, Professor Flora Rheta Schreiber, a significant psychoanalytical scholar, has bequeathed to us the most illuminating study of the mind of the serial killer – a detailed and profound investigation of the early childhood and adolescence of a notorious murderer, Joseph Kallinger, who, in 1974 and 1975, tortured and killed several victims, including one of his own children, while under the influence of persecutory, delusional voices.

Let us examine Professor Schreiber's study of Kallinger with careful consideration.

In 1973, Flora Schreiber (1973) published a landmark book, *Sybil*, about a woman who struggled with multiple personality disorder, and whose illness emerged in the wake of considerable early childhood traumata. Not long thereafter, she expanded her work on the role of adverse life events in the development of psychopathology by arranging to interview a convicted killer, Joseph Kallinger, on numerous occasions over the course of many years. In 1983, she completed her extraordinary study, *The Shoemaker: The Anatomy of a Psychotic* (Schreiber, 1983), whose findings we shall now examine more fully.

Born in Philadelphia, Pennsylvania, in 1935, this future murderer grew up in a stark orphanage, after his mother had abandoned him at only three weeks of age. Eventually, Anna Kallinger, and her husband, Stephen Kallinger, a shoemaker – two childless émigrés from Austria – rescued the young boy and took him into their home. Alas, in spite of having offered the young Joseph shelter, Anna Kallinger – the mother – came to regard her newfound adopted son as a great "disappointment" (Schreiber, 1983, p. 35) and often expressed the regret that she had not selected a female child instead. And Stephen Kallinger – the new father – experienced shame at his own infertility.

This angry couple subjected their adopted child to numerous physical and psychological punishments. At the age of six years, Joseph Kallinger developed a hernia which required an operation. The surgeon inflicted a six-inch scar upon the young boy's body, and he had to remain in hospital for fully sixteen days. Upon returning home, the adoptive parents subjected Joseph Kallinger to a very cruel and perverse experience. They explained that, during the operation, the medical doctor had removed not only the hernia but, also, a demon from inside the boy's penis and that, in consequence, he would never be able to impregnate a girl in later life and that he would always be impotent. Anna Kallinger tormented her young son, "you won't have no demon in *your* bird because your bird will always be small, small, small, small, small!" (quoted in Schreiber, 1983, p. 28). In this respect, the parents had not only inflicted a sadistic threat but, quite unconsciously, had transferred Stephen Kallinger's struggle with infertility onto his adopted son.

Before long, Joseph Kallinger became very preoccupied with knives, fantasising about the implement used by the surgeon, which resembled the one deployed by Stephen Kallinger in his daily work as a shoemaker. Before long, the boy began to experience hallucinations of his severed penis floating on the tip of a knife (Schreiber, 1983).

Kallinger suffered so extensively from this symbolic castration that, years hence, when he engaged in sexual intercourse with a woman, he struggled to achieve an erection, and could do so only by clutching a knife in his hand, which he had secreted near his bed. Suffering as he did from so much sexual impotency and, also, psychological impotency, Kallinger expressed rage whenever he could, not least, by abusing his children. He threw pins at one of his daughters and, also, burned her on the upper thigh with a hot spatula, placed only one quarter of an inch away from her genitals; moreover, he assaulted one of his own sons with a cat-o'-nine-tails and handcuffed him to a refrigerator and, also, chained another of his sons to a bed.

Unsurprisingly, this highly castrated man became profoundly ashamed and viciously angry and, also, delusional, so much so that he came to believe that God had ordered him to kill every single man, woman, and child on the planet. He began by murdering two boys, including one of his own sons. Kallinger then proceeded to execute an innocent woman, whom he tied up and stabbed to death quite viciously, having stuck a knife into her neck at least six times, before eviscerating other parts of her body. During this grisly process, Kallinger became tumescent and then achieved an orgasm.

Naturally, it would be far too simplistic to argue that Kallinger became a murderer as a result of the fact that his parents taunted him with a symbolic castration. Innumerable mothers and fathers have shamed their children throughout human history, yet not all of these victims of emotional abuse have become killers. But Joseph Kallinger endured other extreme traumata. His adoptive parents forced him to pray, while kneeling on sandpaper, causing bruising to his kneecaps. His father beat him all over his body; and his mother hit him on the head with a hammer on several occasions. Furthermore, both father and mother would often thrust their son's hand into the flames of the burner on the kitchen stove as a particularly cruel punishment, designed to expunge the boy of sin.

Joseph Kallinger experienced these horrid physical and emotional tortures not only in his family home but, also, in the local community. During his eighth year, three older boys held him at knife-point and subjected him to fellatio. With such assaults on his body and his mind, Kallinger became enraged, murderously so. Indeed, having endured these multiple traumata, one can certainly appreciate that Kallinger experienced profound death wishes towards his parents, his surgeon and, also, towards the neighbourhood boys.

Having begun to hallucinate and having hatched a psychotic plan to murder the entire human population, Joseph Kallinger certainly became afflicted by an unusually strong "Todeswunsch" – the death wish. Drawing upon the work of Freud, once again, we might also argue that the "Todeswunsch" became greatly exacerbated by the "Kastrationskomplex" (Freud, 1909, p. 3) – castration complex – the fear of being genitally eviscerated and thus rendered impotent, both physically and psychologically.

As a young man, I had the privilege of meeting Professor Flora Rheta Schreiber, the author of *The Shoemaker: The Anatomy of a Psychotic*, whom I had invited to speak at my university. We became friendly, and several years later, during my tenure on an overseas fellowship, Schreiber took me to the Farview State Hospital for the Criminally Insane, in Waymart, Pennsylvania, to meet Joseph Kallinger in person – a chilling experience indeed. Kallinger – lonely and tormented and heavily medicated – sat in a chair and looked rather cadaverous. He adored Flora Schreiber for having taken the trouble to listen to his life story. In many ways, she became the honorary good mother that he had never had.

During my visit with Kallinger in this old-fashioned hospital for the criminally insane, with guards stationed everywhere, and with murderers locked up behind virtually every door, I suddenly began to recall the very first killer that I had ever met, some years previously, namely, "Fred", the diminutive man of 5' 1" whom I described in the "Introduction" to this book. As readers will recall, Fred kindly offered me a tour of the Victorian psychiatric hospital where I had just begun to work, and, to my surprise, I soon discovered that he had shot both his father and his mother in the face.

Although I never worked psychotherapeutically with Fred during my time as a trainee at that hospital, I did come to have many conversations with him and, also, with the other residents on the ramshackle long-stay wards. Fred held the distinction of being the shortest man in the hospital by many, many inches; he also carried himself in a somewhat effeminate manner, so much so that the other male patients used to taunt him and refer to him not as "Fred" but, rather, as "Winifred".

Meeting Joseph Kallinger in an American high-security forensic institution and learning about his early experiences of bodily assault, sexual abuse, and symbolic castration reminded me of Fred, whom I had encountered in that decrepit English psychiatric hospital some years previously. Both had committed vicious murders; and both had endured castration taunts. Unsurprisingly, I began to wonder whether profound attacks upon an individual's sense of potency might contribute to the development of murderousness in later life.

Fred, like Joe Kallinger, had also suffered extreme beatings in childhood from his cruel parents. And, like Kallinger, he experienced castration-related taunts, shamed and laughed at for being regarded as girl-like, rather than as a potent man in own right – more a "Winifred" than a "Fred". Might castration-style experiences offer us a clue to the deeper psychology of certain murderers?

As I began to investigate the subject of castration-related experiences as potential aetiological contributory factors in the history of the male murderer, I discovered that, as early as 1930, the pioneering Hungarian-born psychoanalyst, Dr. Franz Alexander (1930), by that point a stalwart member of the Freudian community in Berlin and a progenitor of psychoanalytical criminology, had testified in the case of a nineteen-year-old lad called "Markus" who had shot and killed both his brother "Wilhelm" and, also, his sibling's friend "Ferdinand" with a revolver. This virtually forgotten essay appeared in a long-extinct German-language periodical, *Die Psychoanalytische Bewegung* [*The Psycho-Analytical Movement*], but it deserves to be remembered for having provided powerful insights into the private life and mind of the killer.

According to Dr. Alexander, the younger brother, Wilhelm, used to thrash his older brother, Markus – the future murderer – in front of family members, which must have evoked considerable feelings of shame and powerlessness, resulting in a tremendous sense of inferiority. Such physical violence among siblings often unfolds in homes in which the children have suffered from deprivation of parental love. According to the family nurse, the mother did not love her boys sufficiently; and Markus, in particular, endured further horrors when, as a three year old, the family called in a physician after having discovered that Markus had begun to masturbate. On the advice of the physician, servants began to watch Markus throughout the night to ensure that he did not stimulate himself. The nurse even threatened him with castration, claiming that, if he continued to massage himself, gypsies would cut off his penis.

Needless to say, one cannot explain a grossly sadistic act of murder as a response to an outdated prohibition against childhood masturbation, but, in the case of this German lad, Markus, he had suffered maternal deprivation, physical abuse, and a castration-style shaming from a doctor and from a servant. With so many people watching his genitals in childhood, he may well have felt very inadequate and impotent; and thus, when, in later years, Markus became angered by the physically abusive brother, his embrace of the phallic-shaped revolver may well have restored a temporary sense of psychological potency.

Perhaps of relevance, it might be worth noting that the infamous Jeffrey Dahmer, the American necrophile and cannibal – one of the most vicious murderers in recent history – first encountered the police after having displayed his genitalia to members of the public at the Wisconsin State Fair, and, subsequently, for masturbating in public near the Kinnickinnic River in

Milwaukee (Masters, 1993), long before his arrest for multiple murders, necrophilia, and necrophagy. Given that most people never expose their private parts at a state fair, or stroke their exposed genitals outdoors, what prompted the twenty-two-year-old Dahmer to have done so? And what connection might his genital exhibitionism have had to his future horrific crimes?

We know that, as a three-year-old boy, Jeffrey Dahmer underwent inguinal hernia surgery, performed through his groin. Might such an experience have contributed to the development of a feeling of castration anxiety, knowing that someone had inserted a sharp knife-like instrument so close to his penis? By having exhibited himself to a crowd of women and children some years later, he would have endeavoured to reassure himself that he still had a sufficiently impactful penis which had the capacity to shock the innocent bystanders.

Of course, not every three-year-old survivor of a hernia operation becomes a flasher and, moreover, a murderer in later years. But Dahmer suffered innumerable other abuses, which contributed to his sense of lack of safety and, consequently, of rage.

Born in 1960, Jeffrey Dahmer grew up in the

home of two parents who quarrelled extensively and who would eventually come to divorce one another. The father – a scientist – spent very little time in the family home, and when he did so, he sometimes attacked his wife physically. The mother – a daughter of an alcoholic father – suffered from profound depression and suicidality, which ultimately resulted in psychiatric hospitalisation.

Jeffrey Dahmer's mother breastfed him for a short while but then weaned him abruptly and, thereafter, bound her breasts so that the boy would no longer have access. Additionally, the young Dahmer had to wear correctional casts on both of his legs for the first four months of his life. While none of these intrafamilial experiences would, in and of themselves, result in the creation of the murderer, such lack of bodily safety and comfort, underpinned by the absence of healthy and attentive parents, would have exacerbated the impact of the invasive surgical hernia procedure which caused tremendous groin pains, and which would have contributed greatly to Dahmer's precarious sense of belonging.

The hernia operation certainly exerted a tremendous impact, both physically and psychologically. The young boy experienced immense pain for at least a week. Dahmer's biographer, Brian Masters (1993, p. 24), who drew upon extensive interview material with this notorious killer, observed, "The deep cut in a sensitive area, the exploration of his inside, all find uncomfortable echoes at a later date. For a very long time, this would be the most intimate event of his life." The impact proved so profound that, years later, Jeffrey Dahmer confessed that, at the time, he thought that the surgeon had actually cut off his genitals in the process and, in consequence, the youngster developed the fantasy that his mother kept his penis and testicles in her possession.

Undoubtedly, Jeffrey Dahmer – unshielded emotionally by his psychologically preoccupied parents – began to act out and, as early as four or five years of age, demonstrated violent behaviours by encouraging a young black boy to stick his hand into a hornet's nest (Smail, 1991).

Furthermore, the family moved house many times during the boy's early years, thus creating a lack of regularity, safety, and security.

And then, in 1966, the mother gave birth to a second baby – also a boy. Not long thereafter, Jeffrey Dahmer, then in his sixth year, began to strangle other boys at school and would be punished with beatings on his rear, administered with a paddle (Masters, 1993). Also, round about that time, this increasingly troubled child would often kill tadpoles – a tell-tale warning sign of incipient murderousness.

Dahmer's mother became increasingly depressed as well; indeed, as a result of both her mental illness and the large doses of sedatives which she imbibed, she often lay on the bed motionless, in corpse-like fashion (Masters, 1993). One can only imagine that Dahmer may have struggled to differentiate between the living and the dead.

By the age of fourteen, Dahmer had begun to drink alcohol on a regular basis (Masters, 1993), thus creating a foundation of even greater disinhibition in later life.

Eventually, Jeffrey Dahmer began to slaughter men and boys – seventeen people in total – and in some instances, he eviscerated the penises and testicles of several of these tragic victims, and he kept these genital parts in his home as macabre trophies. In view of his troubling childhood fantasy that his surgeon had castrated him and that his mother retained his private parts as souvenirs, one can better comprehend

Dahmer's ultimate criminal perversion of eviscerating the genitalia of his victims and preserving them in his home.

It would not be unreasonable to hypothesise that Dahmer experienced himself as a castrated male who needed to knife his victims and cut off their genitalia as a means of making himself feel more potent. And by removing the penises of these innocent men and boys, he turned them into castrated corpses, while he began to experience himself as more empowered.

Strikingly, both Joseph Kallinger and Jeffrey Dahmer endured hernia operations as children. It seems doubtful that most murderers will have undergone similar surgical procedures. But, in my experience, every murderer will have experienced *threats to his or her sense of bodily safety during childhood*, and those who have suffered sexual abuse or physical attacks will have grown up with a deep sense of danger and inadequacy which will be projected into their victims who become the helpless targets of much long-repressed sadism.

It would be folly to suggest that such horrific private experiences as child abuse and psychological attacks on one's sense of potency actually *cause* murder in every instance, but psychoanalytically orientated forensic psychiatrists and other mental health professionals have long recognised the role of humiliation and castration in the genesis of murder. Following in the footsteps of Dr. Franz Alexander, let us recall that, in 1948, the American physician, Dr. Walter Bromberg (1948, p. 163), Senior Psychiatrist at the Bellevue Psychiatric Hospital in New York City, noted that,

> Humiliation centering about lowered social prestige is a common psychological stimulant for crimes of passion. A derogatory remark relating to race, skin color, social position or economic success in life may be sufficient external stimulus to lead the person so singled out into acts of violence. The belittling remark occasions a murderous impulse aimed at removing an intolerable condition, due chiefly to a basic severe sense of inferiority.

Many psychoanalytical practitioners who work daily with murderers have, in fact, come to appreciate the profound impact of these experiences of castration as potential aetiological agents. One need only speak to the distinguished American forensic psychiatrist, Professor James Gilligan (1996, 2001), who has examined an extremely large sample of murderers and who has often reported that, when interviewed closely, killers frequently explain that they had shot or stabbed or strangled their victim because they felt deeply humiliated and shamed in some way. As Gilligan (2016, p. 132) underscored, his patients invariably felt not only humiliated and shamed but, also, "disrespected, dishonored, disgraced, demeaned, defeated, insulted, slighted, rejected, ridiculed, mocked, embarrassed, treated as inferior, unimportant, insignificant or a failure".

Certainly, those of us who work in the field of forensic mental health would all agree that we have never met a single murderer who enjoyed a lovely, peaceful, safe childhood. Such individuals simply do not exist. Murder, though complex in its origins, invariably stems from one or more experiences of trauma, generally of a very severe nature indeed. While many human beings, alas, have experienced sexual abuse, or emotional deprivation, or physical punishment, or threats to their lives, the future murderer will often have endured many, if not all, of these childhood horrors.

One might argue that every human being has experienced some form of rejection, shame, and embarrassment during our earliest years, and that many will also have endured bereavements and punishments; and yet, fewer than one per cent of us actually perpetrate murder. Happily, most of us can survive early traumatic episodes without becoming dangerous lunatics. But those who do so will invariably suffer from a more profound type of abuse and terror, often of a very perverse nature. For instance, Dirk Donovan, an American murderer who multiply stabbed two men to death during a seventy-two-hour period in order to "prove his manhood" (Pincus, 2001, p. 72) to his girlfriend, suffered hugely during his childhood. As a youngster, his mother forced him to perform cunnilingus on her; and his brutal stepfather beat him frequently. On one occasion, the young boy sought safety from his stepfather by climbing up a tree; however, the older man then took an axe and cut down that very tree. Eventually, the parents expelled Dirk Donovan from the family home. The mother later referred to her son as "a stupid, mother-fucking piece of shit" (Pincus, 2001, p. 78). Such parental behaviours cannot be described as normal; even child protection workers would agree that enduring enforced cunnilingus with an adult woman and watching an adult man chopping down a tree in which one has taken refuge cannot be regarded as the ordinary abuses of everyday life.

Unless the forensic patient has an opportunity to discuss his or her personal history in great detail with a trained mental health professional, he or she will often "forget" these early traumata or will be too ashamed to talk about such experiences. Consequently, many killers claim to have little insight into the origins of their cruel behaviours.

After his arrest for multiple murders in 1983, the Englishman Dennis Nilsen met with his solicitor, Ronald Moss, to prepare a defence. Moss asked Nilsen why he had committed so many vicious killings; but Nilsen could offer no coherent explanation, and he simply replied, "I am hoping you will tell me" (quoted in Masters, 1985, p. 24). Nilsen did, however, possess the linguistic capacity to describe himself as an "unhappy, brooding child, secretive and stricken with inferiority" (quoted in Masters, 1985, p. 41). Perhaps the notion of inferiority in a male, which Freud would have conceptualised as castration anxiety, might have some merit. And perhaps, by recognising the deep sense of castration inferiority experienced by our forensic patients from early childhood and adolescence onwards, we might well be able to raise consciousness about this feature of human development and thus contribute, in some small way, towards the prevention of future grotesque crimes.

Some investigators have struggled to ascertain the full cause or causes of murder. For instance, in a study of American female serial killers, several researchers from Penn State Harrisburg, part of Pennsylvania State University, unearthed experiences of physical or sexual abuse – sometimes both – in only 31.5 per cent of the sample (Harrison, Murphy, Ho, Bowers, and Flaherty, 2015). Needless to say, one must wonder about the remaining 68.5 per cent of women who did *not* report abuse. Perhaps these female killers did, indeed, suffer from early assaults that they could not recall consciously, or that, as a result of their characterological oppositionalism, they simply refused to share such private information with their interviewers. But, in any case, the figure of 31.5 per cent must not be readily dismissed, as this still represents a substantial amount of abuse. Nevertheless, one must, however,

wonder whether a group of psychoanalytically orientated clinicians – specially trained to help patients
articulate the most difficult of early traumata over a
longer period of time – might have unearthed an even
higher percentage.

The study of murder – a heaving and unbearable
topic – cannot be confined solely to a consideration
of headline-grabbing serial killers. Some have committed murder in self-defence. And many will have
embarked upon killing sprees without ever having
touched either a knife or a gun. For instance, in Nazi
Germany, Adolf Hitler – to the best of our knowledge – never murdered anyone in a death camp with
his own hands. But, yet, he certainly authorised the
killing of millions. The noted British psychiatrist Dr.
Henry Dicks (1972, p. xi) referred to such people, and
rightly so, as "armchair" murderers.

Even ordinary, law-abiding citizens with no connection to the Nazi movement have caused the deaths
of others, perpetrating what I have come to refer to
as forensic psychopathology of the "sub-clinical" type
(Kahr, 2018d, p. 242), which will never come to the
attention of law enforcement agencies, the criminal
justice system or, indeed, psychiatric services. For

instance, "Mr. J.", a patient whom I assessed years ago – an HIV-positive man who had suffered much physical abuse and trauma during his childhood – would, knowingly, have sex with large numbers of men, and would not inform them of his HIV status beforehand. At least one of these consenting lovers contracted the human immunodeficiency virus and died not long thereafter from the infection (Kahr, 2018d). This sort of unconscious armchair murderer typifies the *ostensibly* non-forensic patient who, nevertheless, causes the death of a fellow human being.

Indeed, hatred of a murderous nature will often excite many people, even on a grossly sexual level. Although the vast majority of adults do not fantasise about murder during lovemaking or during masturbation, we know from the aforementioned British Sexual Fantasy Research Project that a significant number of adults will reach orgasm while thinking about the death of another person (Kahr, 2007, 2008). One need but consider the case of "Yannis", one of my research participants, who confessed that his favourite orgasm-inducing sexual fantasy consists of: "Taking all my enemies, anyone who's ever been cruel to me, and fucking them until they bleed to death" (quoted in Kahr, 2007, p. 336). While we have absolutely no evidence that Yannis ever harmed another person outside his nocturnal fantasies, such erotic thoughts underscore the chilling fact that murder stems from rage and from revenge against cruel perpetrators of unkindness and that the pursuit of murder might even result in sexual pleasure.

Lamentably, we will not cure the world of murder in our lifetime, but I hope that, by acquiring an increased understanding of the role of early traumata, we will become better able to provide more assistance to vulnerable mothers and fathers who struggle with their needy babies. In doing so, we will have an opportunity to reduce the potential for cruelty which often produces dire consequences decades hence.

CONCLUSION
Blue-sky thinking:the future of
forensic mental health

I intend to ſee a Doctor to preſcribe her an
Hour of my Converſation to be taken every
Night and Morning; and this to be
continued till her Fever of Averſion's over.

("Careleſs", in Colley Cibber, *The Double Gallant: Or, the Sick Lady's*
Cure. A Comedy. As it is Acted at the Theatre-Royal in Drury-Lane, by
His Majesty's Servants, 1707, Act I, Scene I [p. 12])

Most visitors to central London will, at some point, pass by Marble Arch, that beautiful, imposing nineteenth-century creation designed by the royal architect John Nash. Upon its completion in 1824, only members of the Royal Family and their troops could pass through this magnificent structure.

However, many centuries previously, the lands surrounding Marble Arch – formerly known as the village of Tyburn – served as the location of innumerable grisly public executions by dissection, hanging, or burning for over 600 years. In fact, as early as 1196, William Fitz Osbern, also known as "Longbeard", suffered death by hanging at Tyburn for having stirred a revolt of merchants to protest the levy of taxes designed to help release Richard, the English king, from Austrian captivity (Bartlett, 2000; Brandon and Brooke, 2007; cf. Marks, n.d. [1908]; Rumbelow, 1982; McKenzie, 2007). In the early eighteenth century, Bernard Mandeville, the Dutch-born philosopher and polemicist, spoke of the "Torrent of Mob" (1725, p. 20) who congregated at Tyburn to watch the "Multitude of unhappy Wretches, that every Year are put to Death for Trifles" (1725, p. [1]), lamenting further, that, "theſe Executions are little better than Barbarity" (p. 36).

Happily, John Nash's imposing arch eventually replaced the gallows – a process which, alas, required more than *six centuries.*

But can we do anything to speed up our understanding of the causes of criminality and, in particular, of the treatment of criminals? Or will we have to wait another 600 years?

Certainly, we no longer chain our dangerous lunatics to the walls of decrepit asylums and we no longer torture them publicly by hanging them from a tree or by decapitating their heads for public spectacle. But what *do* we do with them?

Invariably, we place offender patients in secure psychiatric institutions or in prisons and we frequently ply them with heavy dosages of medication (e.g., Sheard, Marini, Bridges, and Wagner, 1976). This seems a very good idea and, no doubt, each of us sleeps more soundly knowing that our criminal justice system has convicted these paedophiles and murderers and placed them under lock and key, far from our loved ones.

But many psychiatric hospitals and prisons fail to protect the inmates satisfactorily and, often, contribute to further traumatisation; and large numbers of those incarcerated in institutions will be raped (Starchild, 1990), or will perpetrate violent attacks on other patients (Walker and Seifert, 1994) or, indeed, on members of the public (Terranova and Rocca, 2016), or will engage in self-mutilating behaviours (Wray and Eldridge, 1970; Shea, 1993). And many will attack the staff members hired to care for them. According to a recent study of Dutch mental health workers, approximately sixty-seven per cent endured *at least* one episode of violence in the last five years, ranging from being beaten, kicked, stabbed, or bitten, to being sexually assaulted, strangulated or, indeed, having their hair pulled (van Leeuwen and Harte, 2017).

Horrendously, the guards themselves will often commit vicious acts of violence against those in their care. At times, the abuse will be perpetrated by both inmates *and* corrections officers. For instance, quite recently, while transporting a group of prisoners from Rikers Island in New York City to Albany, in upstate New York, a group of guards beat several convicts accused of having assaulted members of staff. According to the victims, the guards pummelled them, used Taser guns on their bodies and, even, inserted not only fingers but, also, batons into their rectums. One nineteen-year-old prisoner, Steven Espinal, suffered hearing loss and, moreover, discovered blood in his urine after beatings by the officers who sentenced him to 600 days of solitary confinement (Ransom, 2018).

The investigative journalist Alisa Roth has published a scathing exposé of the brutality and filth inside American prisons, underscoring that these institutions – heaving with mentally ill offenders – have become the new psychiatric hospitals of our day. As Ms. Roth

(2018, p. 11) has argued, "we continue to treat people with mental illness almost exactly as we did before electricity was invented, before women had the right to vote, and before the abolition of slavery." Having visited multiple prisons, she became appalled by the grotesque physical conditions and by the toxic odour, which she described as "a mix of dirty laundry, un-washed people, and excrement" (Roth, 2018, p. 54).

During a meeting at the Freud Museum London, I found myself discussing Roth's chilling book with several British colleagues who work in prisons on this side of the Atlantic Ocean, each of whom concurred with Roth's assessment. Indeed, one of my co-workers, who consults to prisons on a regular basis, exclaimed that she has never visited a British prison without having seen at least one dead rat lying in the corridors or on the floor of a cell.

On the basis of her searing investigation, Roth (2018, p. 11) has concluded that "locking up vulner-able people in inhumane conditions is fundamentally immoral." Moreover, she has lamented the complete lack of any one-to-one psychotherapy offered to the inmates. In many respects, the prisons of the twen-ty-first century have not progressed beyond those of the medieval era (Bassett, 1943).

The notion of caring for those imprisoned in forensic institutions – whether jails or hospitals – often evokes a great sense of outrage. For instance, in 2017, staff at North Sea Camp, an open prison in the British county of Lincolnshire, began to address the inmates – many of whom had committed gross sexual offences – as "residents" (Ford, 2018, p. 4). Although Mabel Brooks, the chairwoman of the prison's Independent Monitoring Board, claimed that this more humane style of greeting had improved the atmosphere within the institution, Glyn Travis of the Prison Officers' Association objected harshly, complaining, "They are not residents. They are prisoners. The victims of crime would see them as prisoners, not residents" (quoted in Ford, 2018, p. 4).

Certainly, the wish to punish perpetrators of violence by incarcerating them in gross institutions represents not only a conscious wish to protect the public but, also, an unconscious delight to retaliate (Balint, 1951).

But when we treat our prisoners cruelly, we often place ourselves at greater risk.

Back in thirteenth-century Staffordshire, in the

West Midlands region of England, a man called Hugo, who had committed an act of theft, had his head cut off in consequence. After the execution, Hugo's wife, Matilda, full of bitterness and rancour, murdered her three children in desperation (JUST 1/802 (Staffs. 1272), m. 46 dorse (n.d.)). Tragically, punishment invariably breeds further violence.

As we know, when convicted offenders return to the community, they will often perpetrate further crimes, and the rate of recidivism has remained extremely high throughout recorded history (e.g., Seruca and Silva, 2015). According to the Bureau of Justice Statistics of the United States Department of Justice, some *eighty-three per cent* of prisoners released during the year 2005 would come to be rearrested at least once over the next nine years (Alper, Durose, and Markman, 2018). Other nations across the globe have reported similarly worrisome statistics of rearrest and re-conviction and re-imprisonment (Yukhnenko, Sridhar, and Fazel, 2019).

And those who remain incarcerated inside will often kill themselves in acts of desperation. The National Institute for Health and Care Excellence recently reported that offenders in prison will be approximately

8.6 times more likely to commit suicide than members of the general public (*Preventing Suicide in Community and Custodial Settings: NICE Guideline*, 2018; cf. Fazel and Benning, 2009; Marzano, Fazel, Rivlin, and Hawton, 2010; Rivlin, Hawton, Marzano, and Fazel, 2010; Anonymous, 2018). And many female prisoners will have to endure separations from their babies (Wilks-Wiffen, 2011; Powell, Marzano, and Ciclitira, 2017; Powell, Ciclitira, and Marzano, 2017), resulting in bitter consequences for their offspring, who will themselves be at greater risk of becoming violent in later years.

How can we live with ourselves knowing that our nations not only provide so little humane and compassionate treatment for prisoners, but, also, place everyone else at risk due to such negligent treatment?

Today, the vast majority of forensic patients will be incarcerated – often rightly so, in view of their potentiality for becoming dangerous, both to themselves and to others – and they will be heavily medicated with antipsychotic agents, antidepressants, mood stabilisers, benzodiazepines, adrenergic blockers, stimulants, and opiate antagonists (Stahl and Morrissette, 2014). And many will be transported back and forth between custodial settings and psychiatric institutions (e.g., Hill, Mitchell, and Leipold, 2017).

But, in spite of my profound admiration for the brave members of staff at psychiatric and penological institutions, who work with the world's most arguably "evil" men and women on a daily basis, I believe that we might improve the offer and provide much more intensive talking therapies.

Fortunately, in view of the small, but steady, growth of psychoanalytically informed forensic psychotherapy over recent decades, several pioneering colleagues have built upon the foundational ideas of Sigmund Freud and his disciples, and have introduced a more humane psychological attitude into our prisons and forensic psychiatric institutions, in the hope of providing a more advanced and civilised approach to the rehabilitation of those who, as a result of childhood traumata, have committed horrific crimes. Often, the psychoanalyst has the capacity to cure the patient extensively; and sometimes, the clinician will help the forensic patient to sublimate his or her more dangerous expressions of psychopathology, as in the case of Dr. Abraham Brill's (1944) sexual voyeur, who became involved with the law on several occasions and who, after treatment, turned his criminally invasive sexual voyeurism into something far more practical by having become a dealer in optical instruments.

My esteemed teacher, the late Dr. Murray Cox, broke new ground at Broadmoor Hospital, the United Kingdom's leading secure institution – home to many notable multiple murderers – by arranging for members of the Royal Shakespeare Company, including the highly distinguished actor Mark Rylance, to perform the works of the Bard for the inmates (e.g., Cox, 1992b; cf. Cox, 1992a). Dr. Cox, a distinguished Shakespeare scholar in his own right, took immense pleasure in arranging to entertain his patients with some of the best actors in the world and, also, in permitting them to discuss the plays – many of which portray grisly assaults and murders – as part of their psychotherapeutic healing (cf. Black, 2003).

Many other forensic psychotherapists have undertaken similarly creative work. For instance, Paul Kassman devised a project, "Changing the Game", in association with Dr. Carine Minne, at Her Majesty's Prison Grendon, in the village of Grendon Underwood in Buckinghamshire, providing a group psychotherapeutic intervention for convicted, violent gang members – mostly black men from deprived backgrounds. Together, Minne and Kassman (2018) have helped these individuals to work through their early-life abuse and traumata and their long-standing rage, often steeped in racist experiences, by offering sensitive psychological treatment, thus assisting these men to develop more psychological solidity and creativity, so much so that many have subsequently embarked upon more healthy activities, including university study.

Other colleagues have, over the years, actually offered formal psychoanalytically orientated art therapy for prisoners (Collier, 2015, 2019) and, also, psychotherapy (Stewart, 2016a, 2016b, 2019), with encouraging results. Through such work, we have come to learn far more about the ubiquity of trauma in the early histories of offender patients and, also, about their capacity to become repentant, remorseful, and reparative in their state of mind and, perhaps, less likely to perpetrate further crimes after their release from institutions.

Moreover, my colleagues in the field of disability psychotherapy, based at Respond, a pioneering service in London, have, over the years, offered intensive psychoanalytical psychotherapy to those forensic patients who have also struggled with intellectual disabilities and other forms of handicap (e.g., Curen, 2009, 2018; Corbett, 2014). The team at Respond has undertaken an immense amount of work to champion a new subdivision of forensic psychotherapy, now known more widely as *"forensic disability psychotherapy"* (Kahr, 2014a, p. xix; cf. Kahr, 2018b) – a truly creative development of the groundwork established by the founder of contemporary forensic psychotherapy, *Profesora* Estela Welldon (1993, 2011, 2015), and by the progenitor of modern disability psychotherapy, Dr. Valerie Sinason (1992, 1999, 2010).

In the United Kingdom alone, we now boast a Forensic Psychotherapy Society (Kirtchuk, Gordon, Doctor, and Ingram, 2016), which has become a member institution of our national registration body, the British Psychoanalytic Council, as well as a thriving International Association for Forensic Psychotherapy – an organisation with members from all over the world. More recently, this international society has launched specialist training courses in Italy and, also, in Russia and, moreover, has created a new periodical, *The International Journal of Forensic Psychotherapy.*

Over the decades, many forensic mental health

specialists have marginalised, or even mocked, the work of Sigmund Freud and his psychoanalytical colleagues. For instance, in 1936, Dr. William Norwood East (1936, p. 320), then His Majesty's Commissioner of Prisons, and Director of Convict Prisons, not to mention a Lecturer on Crime and Insanity at the Maudsley Hospital in the University of London, expressed derision that a delinquent might be subjected to "hours of compulsory association with a Freudian investigator". Likewise, his contemporary, Dr. Eric Strauss (1939, p. 167), a Physician for Psychological Medicine and a Lecturer in Psychological Medicine at St. Bartholomew's Hospital in London, warned of the potential dangers of "Over-enthusiastic psychotherapists".

More than half a century later, Professor David Canter, arguably the most distinguished forensic psychologist in the United Kingdom, lambasted Freud as "fanciful" (1994, p. 21) and as someone who lumbered us with "ever more elaborate accounts of the underlying mechanisms" (p. 216) of human behaviour.

In more gentlemanly fashion, Professor Michael Gelder, Professor of Psychiatry at the University of Oxford, and his colleagues Dr. Dennis Gath and Dr. Richard Mayou – each a Clinical Reader in Psychiatry at the same institution – dismissed the potential of Freudian insights by explaining, in their landmark and influential *Oxford Textbook of Psychiatry*, "Nowadays it is generally held that social causes of crime are much more important than psychological causes" (Gelder, Gath, and Mayou, 1983, p. 720).

In spite of such condemnations or marginalisations of psychological factors, the psychotherapeutic and psychoanalytical approaches to the understanding of the origins and treatment of criminality have continued to flourish.

Not only have we made advances in exploring the aetiology of dangerous lunacy, but, also, we have made huge strides in rehabilitation through psychoanalytically orientated treatment. Moreover, we have also made considerable contributions to the *prevention* of criminality in the first place through the support of disciplines such as psychodynamically orientated child mental health and couple mental health, endeavouring to prepare mothers and fathers for parenthood before any formal abuse or traumatisation can unfold (Acquarone, 2002, 2004, 2008; Kahr, 2012, 2019; Abse, 2014). For instance, we have already referred to the pioneering work of Dr. Eileen Vizard (1997), who arranged for psychoanalytically orientated assessment and treatment of child and adolescent sexual offenders, providing them with a space to consider their crimes, in the hope of intervening early and thus forestalling the likelihood that they would become career paedophiles in later life.

In the midst of the Second World War, Claud Mullins, a British magistrate, delivered an address to a luncheon sponsored by the Howard League – an organisation that has long championed prison reform. Speaking to his audience, Mullins (1943, p. 141) underscored, "I think we must, for the first few minutes, concentrate on the causes of crime, because you cannot treat people successfully if you do not know what has caused the state which you are trying to cure; and the weakness up to now of penological reform effort has been that it has been rather blind to the causes of crime." Mullins then enumerated what he and his contemporaries in the 1940s considered to be the principal causes of crime, namely, inheritance (i.e., one's genetic vulnerability), poverty, the endocrine glands, as well as lack of parental love, parental separation and divorce, illegitimacy and, also, something that Mullins (1943, p. 143) referred to as "psychological trauma".

This summation from a magistrate offers an indication that crime and violence result from virtually anything and everything ... and perhaps this may be true. But, although we may well come to discover that our genes and our endocrine glands have contributed to the manufacture of murderers, as the decades have unfolded we have certainly accumulated a huge body of data demonstrating that psychological trauma plays an immensely important aetiological role in the development of violent behaviours (e.g., Luntz and Widom, 1994).

The field of neurocriminology continues to prosper (Concannon, 2019; cf. Niehoff, 1999; Rafter, 2008; Haycock, 2014), and understandably so. Previously, we had lacked the necessary technology to investigate the human brain, but now, with functional magnetic resonance imaging and other tools, we have the capacity to see inside the mind much more clearly than ever before. However, in spite of the heroic efforts of these prescient neuroscientists, we have no clear evidence that theft, assault, arson, rape, paedophilia, and murder result directly from brain disorders. We *do* know, however, that violent patients – our dangerous lunatics – have invariably experienced one or more *trauma* during early infancy and childhood and that they have suffered from loss, bereavement, neglect, physical abuse, sexual abuse, or emotional abuse, and, often, from several of these aforementioned psychological pathogens concurrently.

As we indicated in a previous chapter, during the 1930s and 1940s, the great English child psychiatrist and psychoanalyst, Dr. John Bowlby, studied the early lives of young people, aged five to sixteen, who had committed acts of thievery or pilfering and who had become juvenile delinquents. Bowlby (1944a, 1944b, 1945-1946, 1946) and his colleagues examined these aggressive young people and, often, the members of their families with great care, and reconstructed detailed portraits of the early lives of these individuals, some of whom perpetrated acts of great cruelty, such as pushing a young girl off a tricycle or burning a young girl's leg with intention. In virtually every case, these child forensic patients had suffered significant bereavements during their earliest years; indeed, many had lost a mother and, also, at times, a father. Others endured lengthy periods of hospitalisation for various illnesses, resulting in painful deprivations of maternal affection during critical stages of development.

One of the children who participated in Bowlby's (1944a, 1944b) study, a young thief called "Edward G.L.", the ninth of eleven children, suffered from a chronic depression, having endured extreme deprivations and bereavements throughout his early years. During Edward's fifth year, his father died in a railway accident; and then, some seven years later, during the boy's twelfth year, his mother died from consumption. Another one of the children in this study, "Audrey H.", had to endure, at approximately seven years of age, the death of her beloved grandmother, followed not long thereafter by the shocking death of her five-year-old brother, run over by a lorry in Audrey's presence. It did not surprise Bowlby (1944a, 1944b) that, by the age of ten, Audrey began to steal coins from the pockets of her school mates.

Some of the youngsters in Bowlby's (1944a, 1944b) research project had to navigate even more tragic histories, such as "Arthur L.", an illegitimate child, born to a mother who worked in a tavern, impregnated by the publican whom she barely knew. Arthur spent little time with his mother during his infancy as she had despatched him to live with various relatives. Indeed, during the first nine years of his life, Arthur's mother saw him merely on a fortnightly basis and boasted that

Arthur had had to rear himself. Eventually, Arthur became a childhood thief and a truant. In a subsequent publication, Bowlby (1945-1946, p. 33) characterised Arthur thus: "I have never seen a more isolated boy. I do not think I have ever had the experience of talking to a brick wall so vividly as with this boy over a long period. In fact, I never made any contact with him at all, nor did anyone else."

Such traumata of separation, neglect, and loss proved to be rather commonplace, if not omnipresent, in the early life histories of those boys and girls who ultimately became thieves. Needless to say, not every child who has experienced bereavement will become a criminal, but many will have done, underscoring that loss places young people at considerable risk.

During the nineteenth century, delinquent children would be subjected to whipping, imprisonment, and neglect (Duckworth, 2002), not to mention confinement in a workhouse and, even, transportation abroad (Shore, 1999). But, Bowlby and his team of colleagues progressed beyond these cruel interventions by having provided psychological treatment for many of these criminal children in the hope of preventing them from becoming career offenders in later life.

Such early forensic psychotherapeutic interventions represented a great advance in the history of humanity.

Through his pioneering studies, John Bowlby laid the foundations for an understanding of the role of early trauma and deprivation in the development of criminality. For instance, more than forty years later, two psychopathology researchers, Dr. Matti Huttunen and Dr. Pekka Niskanen (1978), undertook an intensive investigation of the Finnish population registers from 1925 to 1957, and discovered that patients who had perpetrated crimes had lost their fathers before birth far more frequently than members of a control group. Trauma certainly places men and women at significant risk of developing criminality in later life.

In the preceding chapters, I have offered a brief survey of some of the well-known and, also, neglected gems from the psychoanalytical literature which demonstrate the powerful role of loss and deprivation, abuse and cruelty, and trauma of all varieties in the early life histories of future delinquents, paedophiles, and murderers. Trauma has certainly scarred the biography of every single forensic patient with whom I have ever worked. For instance, those who set fire to buildings, namely, arsonists, have also experienced considerable impingements in early life. Dr. Lynn Stewart (1993), a psychologist at Her Majesty's Prison Holloway in London, discovered that many female arsonists had come from broken homes and that as many as sixty-two per cent had suffered from sexual assaults. In a subsequent study, three London-based psychiatrists, Dr. Basant Puri, Dr. Richard Baxter, and Dr. Christopher Cordess (1995), confirmed the frequency of sexual abuse in the histories of fire-setters and, also, noted that many had endured early bereavements and social isolation as well. Thus, psychosocial trauma represents a potentially ubiquitous feature in the backgrounds of forensic patients – dangerous lunatics – of every shape and size (cf. Bhatia, Srivastava, Khyati, and Kaushik, 2016). Even the most conservative and biologically orientated periodicals, such as *Psychological Medicine*, published by Cambridge University Press, have begun to recognise the role of traumatogenesis in the development of criminality (e.g., Augsburger, Basler, and Maercker, 2019). And we owe this recognition predominantly to Sigmund Freud and to his numerous followers who came to specialise in forensic psychotherapy. Regrettably, traditional psychiatry has taken rather a long time to appreciate such insights.

Over the course of human history, we have treated offenders – even those suffering from mental distress or mental illness – with profound cruelty. Often, those who have inflicted legal punishments have committed far more ghastly acts than those incarcerated for their crimes. Fortunately, in spite of our dreadful track record, a few glimmers of humanitarian light have begun to appear upon the horizon in recent decades. And psychoanalytical mental health professionals, in particular, have made important contributions in this respect.

Once we come to appreciate that crime results predominantly from early trauma and loss, rather than from bad genes or from a "neurotic taint" (Levy, 1932, p. 76), we will be much better able to offer appropriate assistance to those who have perpetrated offences, namely, humane containment in psychologically sophisticated institutions, where indicated, combined with intensive psychotherapy designed to prevent the likelihood of recidivism. When I began to train, the phrase "forensic psychotherapy" barely existed. But now, decades later, we have the possibility of providing a more enlightened form of relief to the dangerous lunatics in our midst.

We still have much work to accomplish in this

respect. Recently, the distinguished publication *Criminology and Public Policy* – the journal of the American Society of Criminology – devoted a special section to "Juveniles' Right to Counsel" (Bishop, 2010; Feld and Schaefer, 2010; Kempf-Leonard, 2010; Schwartz and Levick, 2010). Although we all support the basic right of troubled juveniles to receive appropriate legal counsel, I could not help but wish that such young offenders should one day be offered not only *counsel* but, also, *counselling*. Only by helping these criminals to work through the early traumatic roots of their forensic behaviours will we be able to humanise those who have become grossly dehumanised.

Let us conclude these brief remarks with reference to two of the most impactful people of modern times, namely, the Nazi dictator Adolf Hitler and the psychoanalyst Melanie Klein.

In the second chapter of the second volume of Hitler's (1927 [1926], p. 478) notorious tract, *Mein Kampf*, he ranted at reports that a black-skinned person – a "Neger" (the German word for "Negro") – might have the temerity to become a lawyer, a teacher, a priest or, even, an opera singer. He then expressed his deep concern and horror that Jews might, misguidedly, come to regard such achievements as evidence of human equality. As Hitler (1927 [1926], p. 479) explained, "daß es ein verbrecheriſcher Wahnwitz iſt, einen geborenen Halbaffen ſo lange zu dreſſieren, bis man glaubt, aus ihm einen Advokaten gemacht zu haben", which we might translate as, "it is criminal madness to train a born semi-ape man long enough to believe that he has been made a lawyer."

Through his use of the phrase "verbrecheriſcher Wahnwitz" – "criminal madness" – Adolf Hitler had, quite unwittingly, drawn upon a long historical tradition within medicine, and psychiatry in particular, of dismissing most criminals as lunatics. By evoking this nineteenth-century notion of dangerous lunacy, Hitler, in his chilling fashion, dismissed anyone that he hated as little more than a crazy person, thus justifying treatment of the most sadistic nature. In view of Hitler's subsequent sanction of the murder of multiple millions of innocent people, one might argue that he had projected his own criminal madness and his own dangerous lunacy onto the men, women, and children who became his victims.

Fortunately, psychoanalytical practitioners and other mental health specialists have worked hard over

the last century to champion a more profound understanding of the traumatic roots of dangerous lunacy
and, also, a more compassionate approach to treatment
and care.

Back in 1932, Melanie Klein, one of the progenitors of child psychoanalysis, argued passionately
that, if mental health practitioners could intervene
early on in the life cycle of a young person, and could
provide psychological treatment, one might, thereby,
be able to prevent future breakdown, hospitalisation,
and, even, imprisonment. As Klein (1932b, p. 374)
exclaimed, "If every child who shows disturbances
that are at all severe were to be analysed in good time,
a great number of those people who later end up in
prisons or lunatic asylums, or who go completely to
pieces, would be saved from such a fate and be able
to develop a normal life."[8]

The criminally insane have haunted humanity
since time immemorial. Indeed, "Claudius King of
Denmarke", one of the principal characters in William
Shakespeare's play *The Tragedie of Hamlet, Prince of
Denmarke*, spoke of "turbulent and dangerous Lunacy"
(Act III, Scene i, line 4). And yet, in spite of centuries
of medical and criminological investigation, we have

made little progress in the cure of such individuals, until, I believe, the discovery and development of both dynamic psychology and traumatogenesis.

We have now harvested, I hope, enough evidence to suggest that trauma plays a significant role in the genesis of criminality. We have also accumulated considerable data over more than one century, confirming that intensive psychological treatment truly facilitates cure. Consequently, we now have the opportunity to apply this knowledge on a much wider canvas, and by doing so, we might make a real improvement to our utterly too, too violent world.

END NOTES

1. Unless otherwise indicated, the author must assume responsibility for the translation of all passages and phrases from French, German, and Italian.

2. In his biography of the Athenian statesman Solon, one of the many *Vitae Parallelae* [*Parallel Lives*], the ancient Greek essayist Plutarch (Plvtarchi [Plutarch], n.d., p. 349) wrote, "Vnde poſtmodum lepide ait Demades, ſanguine Draconem, non atramento, ſcripſiſſe leges." This phrase translates thus: "So that Demades, in after time, was thought to have said very happily, that Draco's laws were written not with ink, but blood" (Plutarch, n.d., p. 184).

3. William Shakespeare's play about the life of Richard, the duke of Gloucester, first appeared under the title: *The Tragedy of King Richard the third: Containing, His treacherous Plots againſt his brother Clarence: the pittiefull murther of his innocent nephewes: his tyrannicall vſurpation: with the*

whole courſe of his deteſted life, and moſt deſerued death. As it hath beene lately Acted by the Right honourable the Lord Chamberlaine his ſeruants.

4. For these quotations from the work of William Shakespeare, I have relied upon the very first folio edition of his collected writings, *Mr. William Shakespeares Comedies, Histories, & Tragedies. Publiſhed according to the True Originall Copies,* first printed in London in 1623.

5. The original German sentence reads: "Ich könnte zum Beispiel den Satz nicht unterschreiben, daß die Behandlung der Strafgefangenen eine Schande für unsere Kultur ist. Im Gegenteil, würde mir eine Stimme sagen: sie ist ganz in Einklang mit unserer Kultur, notwendige Äußerung der Brutalität und des Unverstandes, die die gegenwärtige Kultur-menschheit beherrschen" (Freud, 1931a, p. x).

6. This Indian psychoanalyst would sometimes spell his name as Girindrashekhar Bose.

7. The original French passage reads: "Sept fois sur treize il s'agissait d'une liaison infantile des deux côtés, de rapports sexuels entre une petite fille et un garçon un peu plus âgé, le plus souvent son frère, et lui-même victime d'une séduction antérieure. Ces

liaisons s'étaient continuées quelquefois pendant des années jusqu'à la puberté des petits coupables, le garçon répétant toujours et sans innovation sur la petite fille les mêmes pratiques, qu'il avait subi lui-même de la part d'une servante ou gouvernante, et qui pour cause de cette origine étaient souvent de nature dégoutante. Dans quelques cas il y avait concurrence d'attentat et de liaison infantile, ou abus brutal réitéré" (Freud, 1896a, p. 167).

8. The original German text reads: "Würde jedes Kind, das ernstere Störungen zeigt, rechtzeitig der Analyse unterzogen, dann könnte wohl ein großer Teil jener Menschen, die andernfalls in Gefängnissen und Irrenhäusern landen oder sonst völlig scheitern, vor diesem Schicksal bewahrt bleiben und sich zu normalen Menschen entwickeln" (Klein, 1932a, p. 293).

ACKNOWLEDGEMENTS

I wish to express my deepest thanks to some of my most influential teachers and mentors in the field of forensic mental health, including, the late Dr. Murray Cox, the late Dr. Susanna Isaacs Elmhirst, Dr. Judith Freedman, the late Dr. Mervin Glasser, Dr. Elif Gürisik, the late Dr. Brendan MacCarthy, Dr. Valerie Sinason, Dr. Eileen Vizard, CBE, *Profesora* Estela Welldon, and others too numerous to mention, as well as my many friends and colleagues and students in the forensic psychotherapy community from whom I have learned so much over the years.

I owe immense gratitude and appreciation to Jane Ryan, the founder and Chief Executive Officer of Confer, whose landmark work as the progenitor of this remarkable organisation has helped to disseminate solid and cutting-edge mental health knowledge throughout the United Kingdom and beyond. I also wish to convey my admiration of the collegial and gentlemanly Dr. Joel Oberstar and Dr. Stephen Setterberg – each a fellow Director of Confer – whose creativity and facilitation has helped to launch Confer Books, with the inspiring Dr. Setterberg as our Publisher. Dr. Rod Tweedy, the former Senior Commissioning Editor, has proved to be a magnificent supporter and an intelligent pair of eyes and ears throughout the publication process, as have Todd Archbold, Suzy Lucas, Christina Wipf Perry, Dr. Kathy Rooney, and Liz Wilson.

I must also thank the other members of the Confer team including, Richard Atienza-Hawkes, Rebekah Ball, Julie Bennett, Josh Daniel, Kieran Falconer, Jenny Keen, Sheila Kibukamusoke, Cressida Moger, Ryan Murphy, Donna Redmond, Louise Smith, Alice Waterfall, and Helen Whitehorn for their wisdom and comradeship. I also extend my warm appreciation to Jamie Keenan of Keenan Design for his wonderful book cover. As ever, I wish to convey my deep appreciation to the meticulous James Darley for his sterling work as copy-editor.

A scholar cannot write without the support of a great number of magnificent libraries and archives. I wish to offer my immense appreciation to the numerous dedicated specialist librarians and archivists and other staff members who have assisted me with my historical researches, including, Robert Greenwood and his helpful colleagues at the Members' Library at the Royal Society of Medicine in London, as well as the staff at the Wellcome Library in London and, of course, Daniel Bento, Francisco da Silva, Bryony Davies, Sophie Leighton, Carol Seigel, Ivan Ward, and all of the other gracious members of the team at the Freud Museum London. Furthermore, I wish to express my long-standing fondness to the staff at the Library of the Tavistock Centre and, also, at the British Library. And, of course, I could not have completed this work without the wonderful privilege of my membership in the London Library; and I express my sincere thanks to those staff members who granted me permission to study some of the rare eighteenth-century treatises on crime and punishment, stored in the library's safe.

I have adapted portions of Chapter 3 and Chapter 4 from my previously published essay on the history of forensic psychoanalysis (Kahr, 2018c), which appeared in a Festschrift which I edited in honour of my esteemed teacher, *Profesora* Estela Valentina Welldon (Kahr, 2018a). I first presented a much-foreshortened version of Chapter 6 at a panel discussion on "Criminal Minds", sponsored jointly by *The International Journal of Psychoanalysis*, in celebration of its one hundredth

birthday, and Media and the Inner World, held, fit-
tingly, in the Sigmund Freud Room at the Institute
of Psychoanalysis in London. I wish to thank the or-
ganisers, Professor Caroline Bainbridge and Professor
Candida Yates, and, also, my fellow panellist, Dr. Rachel
Cohen, for their helpful comments and, likewise, Dr.
Cleo Van Velsen, who offered a most useful insight
on that occasion. Moreover, I extend my gratitude to
Dr. Dana Birksted-Breen, the Editor-in-Chief of the
journal, for her warm encouragement.

A number of cherished colleagues took the
trouble to read the typescript of this book prior to
publication. Raffaella Hilty, a brilliant former student
and, now, a brilliant colleague, commented upon the
entire text with great care, as did several esteemed
forensic colleagues, including, Jessica Collier, an Editor
of *The International Journal of Forensic Psychotherapy*;
Richard Curen, Chair of the Forensic Psychotherapy
Society; and Dr. Carine Minne, President of the International Association for Forensic Psychotherapy and,
also, an Editor of our new forensic periodical. Each of
these deeply experienced forensic mental health specialists combed through the typescript with meticulous
attention to detail and with creative engagement, for
which I remain most thankful. And the grandmother

of our profession, *Profesora* Estela Welldon, to whom I owe a lifetime of debt, and without whom I might never have immersed myself in forensic matters at all, read the typescript with immediacy and with care, and then offered much encouragement and many insightful comments as well as a flood of captivating memories of her own early days in the trenches.

I wish to convey my warmest thanks to my dear friend Dan Chambers. During the writing of this book, Dan produced a magnificent documentary for the British television network ITV, *Fred & Rose West: The Real Story with Trevor McDonald*, about the lives of two notorious multiple murderers, which contained vital new information about this chilling case. As a result of my regular conversations with Dan Chambers about the psychology of violence, I learned a great deal and I certainly sharpened my thinking.

As ever, I wish to express my love and appreciation to my family for their encouragement throughout the writing of this book.

REFERENCES

Abel, Gene G., and Osborn, Candice A. (1996). Behavioural
Therapy Treatment for Sex-Offenders. In Ismond Rosen (Ed.).
Sexual Deviation: Third Edition, pp. 382-398. Oxford: Oxford
University Press.

Abraham, Karl (1924). Letter to Sigmund Freud. 25th May. In
Sigmund Freud and Karl Abraham (2009). *Briefwechsel 1907-
1925: Vollständige Ausgabe. Band 2: 1915-1925.* Ernst Falzeder
and Ludger M. Hermanns (Eds.), pp. 765-766. Vienna: Verlag
Turia und Kant.

Abrahams, Vivian C., Hilton, Sidney M., and Zbrozẏna, Andrzej
W. (1964). The Role of Active Muscle Vasodilatation in the
Alerting Stage of the Defence Reaction. *Journal of Physiology*,
171, 189-202.

Abse, Susanna (2014). Psychoanalysis, the Secure Society and the
Role of Relationships. *Psychoanalytic Psychotherapy*, 28, 295-
303.

Acquarone, Stella (2002). Mother-Infant Psychotherapy: A Classi-
fication of Eleven Psychoanalytic Treatment Strategies. In Brett
Kahr (Ed.). *The Legacy of Winnicott: Essays on Infant and Child
Mental Health*, pp. 50-78. London: H. Karnac (Books) / Other
Press.

Acquarone, Stella (2004). *Infant-Parent Psychotherapy: A Hand-
book.* London: H. Karnac (Books).

Acquarone, Stella M. (2008). Violence and Babies. In Rosemary
Campher (Ed.). *Violence in Children: Understanding and Helping Those Who Harm*, pp. 95-127. London: Karnac Books.

Adshead, Gwen (2016). Making Minds More Secure: Remember-
ing Gill McGauley. *Psychoanalytic Psychotherapy*, 30, 298-299.

Adshead, Gwen (2018). Mothers-in-Law: Maternal Function
and Child Protection. In Brett Kahr (Ed.). *New Horizons in
Forensic Psychotherapy: Exploring the Work of Estela V. Welldon*,
pp. 110-123. London: Karnac Books.

Adshead, Gwen, and Mezey, Gillian (1993). Ethical Issues in the
Psychotherapeutic Treatment of Paedophiles: Whose Side Are

References

You On? *Journal of Forensic Psychiatry*, 4, 361-368.

Aichhorn, August (1925). *Verwahrloste Jugend: Die Psychoanalyse in der Fürsorgeerziehung. Zehn Vorträge zur ersten Einführung.* Vienna: Internationaler Psychoanalytischer Verlag.

Aichhorn, August (1932). Treatment Versus Punishment in the Management of Juvenile Delinquents. Frederick M. Sallagar (Transl.). In *Proceedings of the First International Congress on Mental Hygiene: Volume One*, pp. 582-598. New York: International Committee for Mental Hygiene.

Aichhorn, Thomas (2014). "Ein Schuß gegen den Vater. Attentat eines Studenten": Sigmund Freud und der "Fall Ernst Haberl". *Luzifer-Amor*, 27, Number 53, 108-121.

Alabaster, Ernest (1899). *Notes and Commentaries on Chinese Criminal Law and Cognate Topics: With Special Relation to Ruling Cases. Together with a Brief Excursus on the Law of Property Chiefly Founded on the Writings of the Late Sir Chaloner Alabaster, K.C.M.G., etc., Sometime H.B.M. Consul-General in China.* London: Luzac and Company.

Alexander, Franz (1925). Psychoanalytischen Gutachten vor Gericht. *Internationale Zeitschrift für Psychoanalyse*, 11, 128-129.

Alexander, Franz (1930). Der Doppelmord eines 19jährigen. *Die psychoanalytische Bewegung*, 2, 80-93.

Alexander, Franz (1931a). Psychische Hygiene und Kriminalität. *Imago*, 17, 145-173.

Alexander, Franz (1931b). Ein besessener Autofahrer: Ein psychoanalytischen Gutachten. *Imago*, 17, 174-193.

Alexander, Franz, and Healy, William (1935). *Roots of Crime: Psychoanalytic Studies.* New York: Alfred A. Knopf.

Alexander, Franz, and Staub, Hugo (1929). *Der Verbrecher und seine Richter: Ein psychoanalytischer Einblick in die Welt der Paragraphen.* Vienna: Internationaler Psychoanalytischer Verlag.

Alexander, Ilonka Venier (2019). Personal Communication to the Author. 18th February.

Alper, Joseph S. (1995). Biological Influences on Criminal Behaviour: How Good is the Evidence? Available Studies Have Their Limitations. *British Medical Journal.* 4th February, pp. 272-273.

Alper, Mariel; Durose, Matthew R., and Markman, Joshua (2018). *2018 Update on Prisoner Recidivism: A 9-Year Follow-up Period*

References

(2005-2014). Washington, D.C.: Bureau of Justice Statistics, Office of Justice Programs, U.S. Department of Justice. Bureau of Justice Statistics. [https://www.bjs.gov/content/pub/pdf/18upr9yfup0514.pdf; Accessed on 9th March, 2019].

Anonymous (1863). Dangerous Classes. *Medical Critic and Psychological Journal*, 3, 136-154.

Anonymous (1864). The Case of Dr. David M. Wright: For the Murder of Lieutenant Sanborn – Plea, Insanity. *American Journal of Insanity*, 20, 284-300.

Anonymous (1868). Case of Mrs. Elizabeth Heggie. *American Journal of Insanity*, 25, 1-51.

Anonymous (1871). The McFarland Trial. *American Journal of Insanity*, 27, 265-273.

Anonymous (1926). Indian Psycho-Analytical Society: Annual Report, 1925, pp. 291-293. In Max Eitingon (Ed.). *Bulletin of the International Psycho-Analytical Association. International Journal of Psycho-Analysis*, 7, 285-295.

Anonymous (1970). Neurosurgery for the Paedophilic Homosexual. *World Medicine*, 6, Number 4. 11th November, pp. 42-43, 45.

Anonymous (1995). Personal Communication to the Author. 19th February.

Anonymous (2018). Suicide in Prisons: NICE Fights Fires. *The Lancet*. 10th March – 16th March, p. 912.

Augsburger, Mareike; Basler, Kayley, and Maercker, Andreas (2019). Is There a Female Cycle of Violence After Exposure to Childhood Maltreatment?: A Meta-analysis. *Psychological Medicine*, 49, 1776-1786.

Balint, Michael (1951). On Punishing Offenders. In George B. Wilbur, Warner Muensterberger, and Lottie M. Maury (Eds.). *Psychoanalysis and Culture: Essays in Honor of Géza Róheim*, pp. 254-279. New York: International Universities Press.

Bartlett, Robert (2000). *England Under the Norman and Angevin Kings: 1075-1225*. Oxford: Clarendon Press / Oxford University Press.

Bassett, Margery (1943). Newgate Prison in the Middle Ages. *Speculum*, 18, 233-246.

Bates, Victoria (2016). *Sexual Forensics in Victorian and Edwardian England: Age, Crime and Consent in the Courts*. Houndmills, Basingstoke, Hampshire: Palgrave Macmillan / Macmillan Publishers.

References

Beccaria, Cesare (1764). *Dei delitti e delle pene*. Brescia: Nicoló Bettoni, 1807.

Belke, Ingrid (1978). *Die sozialreformerischen Ideen von Josef Popper-Lynkeus: (1838-1921). Im Zusammenhang mit allgemeinen Reformbestrebungen des Wiener Bürgertums um die Jahrhundertwende*. Tübingen: J.C.B. Mohr (Paul Siebeck).

Berlins, Marcel (1986). Portrait of a Serial Killer. *The Times*. 28th July, p. 10.

Bertin, Célia (1982). *La Dernière Bonaparte*. Paris: Librairie Académique Perrin.

Bhatia, Manjeet Singh; Srivastava, Shruti; Khyati, Meghashyam, and Kaushik, Rohit (2016). Prevalence of Abuse in Mentally Ill Patients Visiting Outpatient Setting in a Tertiary Care Hospital in India. *Medicine, Science and the Law*, 56, 91-98.

Bishop, Donna M. (2010). Juvenile Law Reform: Ensuring the Right to Counsel. *Criminology and Public Policy*, 9, 321-325.

Black, D. Anthony (2003). *Broadmoor Interacts: Criminal Insanity Revisited. A Sequel to Partridge's 'Broadmoor: A History of Criminal Lunacy and its Problems' for the Period Between the Mental Health Acts of 1959 and 1983 and a Psychological Perspective on its Clinical Development*. Chichester, West Sussex: Barry Rose Law Publishers.

Bluglass, Robert, and Bowden, Paul (Eds.). (1990). *Principles and Practice of Forensic Psychiatry*. Edinburgh: Churchill Livingstone / Medical Division of Longman Group UK.

Bose, Girindrashekhar (1945). *Everyday Psycho-Analysis*. Calcutta: Susil Gupta.

Bowen-Rowlands, Ernest (1924). *Judgment of Death*. London: W. Collins Sons and Company.

Bowlby, John (1944a). Forty-Four Juvenile Thieves: Their Characters and Home-Life. *International Journal of Psycho-Analysis*, 25, 19-53.

Bowlby, John (1944b). Forty-Four Juvenile Thieves: Their Characters and Home-Life (II). *International Journal of Psycho-Analysis*, 25, 107-128.

Bowlby, John (1945-1946). Childhood Origins of Recidivism. *Howard Journal*, 7, 30-33.

Bowlby, John (1946). *Forty-Four Juvenile Thieves: Their Characters and Home-Life*. Covent Garden, London: Baillière, Tindall and Cox.

Bowlby, John (1951a). *Maternal Care and Mental Health: A Report Prepared on Behalf of the World Health Organization as a Contribution to the United Nations Programme for the Welfare of Homeless Children.* Geneva: World Health Organization.

Bowlby, John (1951b). *Maternal Care and Mental Health. Bulletin de l'Organisation Mondiale de la Santé / Bulletin of the World Health Organization*, 3, 355-533.

Brandon, David, and Brooke, Alan (2007). *Marylebone and Tyburn Past.* London: Historical Publications.

Bremer, Johan (1959). *Asexualization: A Follow-up Study of 244 Cases.* New York: Macmillan Company.

Breuer, Josef (1895). Beobachtung I. Frl. Anna O ... In Josef Breuer and Sigmund Freud. *Studien über Hysterie*, pp. 15-37. Vienna: Franz Deuticke.

Brill, Abraham A. (1944). *Freud's Contribution to Psychiatry.* New York: W.W. Norton and Company.

Bromberg, Walter (1948). *Crime and the Mind: An Outline of Psychiatric Criminology.* Philadelphia, Pennsylvania: J.B. Lippincott Company Publishers.

Brooks, John H., and Reddon, John R. (1996). Serum Testosterone in Violent and Nonviolent Young Offenders. *Journal of Clinical Psychology*, 52, 475-483.

Brouardel, Paul (1897). *L'Infanticide.* Paris: Librairie J.-B. Baillière et Fils.

Brouardel, Paul (1909). *Les Attentats aux moeurs.* Paris: Librairie J.-B. Baillière et Fils.

Brown, Isaac Baker (1866). *On the Curability of Certain Forms of Insanity, Epilepsy, Catalepsy, and Hysteria in Females.* London: Robert Hardwicke.

Brown, Theodore M. (1987). Alan Gregg and the Rockefeller Foundation's Support of Franz Alexander's Psychosomatic Research. *Bulletin of the History of Medicine*, 61, 155-182.

Bruce, Frederick (1872). Letter to Victoria. 1st March. In Victoria (1926). *The Letters of Queen Victoria: Second Series. A Selection from Her Majesty's Correspondence and Journal Between the Years 1862 and 1878. Published by Authority of His Majesty the King. In Two Volumes. Vol. II. 1870-1878.* George Earle Buckle (Ed.), pp. 200-201. London: John Murray.

Burg, B. Richard (2007). *Boys at Sea: Sodomy, Indecency, and Courts Martial in Nelson's Navy.* Houndsmills, Basingstoke, Hampshire: Palgrave Macmillan / Palgrave Macmillan Division of St. Martin's Press.

Burrage, Henry Sweetser (1906). *Gettysburg and Lincoln: The Battle, the Cemetery, and the National Park.* New York: G.P. Putnam's Sons / Knickerbocker Press.

Campbell, Donald (1994). Breaching the Shame Shield: Thoughts on the Assessment of Adolescent Child Sexual Abusers. *Journal of Child Psychotherapy*, 20, 309-326.

Canter, David (1994). *Criminal Shadows: Inside the Mind of the Serial Killer.* Hammersmith, London: HarperCollins Publishers.

Cassity, John Holland (1927). Psychological Considerations of Pedophilia. *Psychoanalytic Review*, 14, 189-199.

Cawthorne, Nigel (2006). *Public Executions.* London: Arcturus / Arcturus Publishing Company, and Cippenham, Slough, Berkshire: Foulsham / W. Foulsham and Company.

Childs, Jessie (2014). *God's Traitors: Terror and Faith in Elizabethan England.* London: Bodley Head / Random House, Random House Group.

Church, Archibald (1893). Removal of Ovaries and Tubes in the Insane and Neurotic. *American Journal of Obstetrics and Diseases of Women and Children*, 28, 491-498.

Cibber, Colley (1707). *The Double Gallant: Or, the Sick Lady's Cure. A Comedy. As it is Acted at the Theatre-Royal in Drury-Lane, by His Majesty's Servants.* London: Henry Lintot, 1736. In Colley Cibber (1736). *The Dramatick Works of Colley Cibber, Efq; Volume IV. Containing, Double Gallant. Refusal. Caesar in Aegypt. Xerxes,* pp. [3]-[96]. London: W. Feales.

Claridge, Mary (1966). *Margaret Clitherow (1556?-1586).* London: Burns and Oates.

Clarke, Charles K. (1886). The Case of William B. – Moral Imbecility. *American Journal of Insanity*, 43, 83-103.

Clouston, Thomas S. (1870). "The McFarland Trial.". *Journal of Mental Science*, 16, 420-424.

Cohn, Haim Hermann (1971). Capital Punishment. In *Encyclopaedia Judaica: Volume 5. C-Dh,* pp. 142-145. Jerusalem: Encyclopaedia Judaica / Keter Publishing House.

Colaizzi, Janet (1989). *Homicidal Insanity, 1800-1985.* Tuscaloosa, Alabama: University of Alabama Press.

Collier, Jessica (2015). 3 Man Unlock: Out of Sight, Out of Mind. Art Psychotherapy with a Woman with Severe and Dangerous Personality Disorder in Prison. *Psychoanalytic Psychotherapy*, 29, 243-261.

Collier, Jessica (2019). Trauma, Art and the "Borderspace": Working with Traumatic Re-enactments. In Pamela Windham Stewart and Jessica Collier (Eds.). *The End of the Sentence: Psychotherapy with Female Offenders*, pp. 164-182. London: Routledge / Taylor and Francis Group, and Abingdon, Oxfordshire: Routledge / Taylor and Francis Group.

Concannon, Diana M. (2019). *Neurocriminology: Forensic and Legal Applications, Public Policy Implications*. Boca Raton, Florida: CRC Press / Taylor and Francis Group.

Conolly, John (1856). *The Treatment of the Insane without Mechanical Restraints*. London: Smith, Elder and Company.

Cooper, George (1994). *Lost Love: A True Story of Passion, Murder, and Justice in Old New York*. New York: Pantheon Books / Random House.

Corbett, Alan (2014). *Disabling Perversions: Forensic Psychotherapy with People with Intellectual Disabilities*. London: Karnac Books.

Coventry, Charles B. (1844). Medical Jurisprudence of Insanity. *American Journal of Insanity*, 1, 134-144.

Cox, Murray (Ed.). (1992a). *Shakespeare Comes to Broadmoor: 'The Actors are Come Hither'. The Performance of Tragedy in a Secure Psychiatric Hospital*. London: Jessica Kingsley Publishers.

Cox, Murray (1992b). Forensic Psychiatry and Forensic Psychotherapy. In Murray Cox (Ed.). *Shakespeare Comes to Broadmoor: 'The Actors Are Come Hither'. The Performance of Tragedy in a Secure Psychiatric Hospital*, pp. 253-258. London: Jessica Kingsley Publishers.

Curen, Richard (2009). 'Can They See in the Door?': Issues in the Assessment and Treatment of Sex Offenders Who Have Intellectual Disabilities. In Tamsin Cottis (Ed.). *Intellectual Disability, Trauma and Psychotherapy*, pp. 90-113. London: Routledge / Taylor and Francis Group, and Hove, East Sussex: Routledge / Taylor and Francis Group.

Curen, Richard (2018). Responses to Trauma, Enactments of Trauma: The Psychodynamics of an Intellectually Disabled Family. In Brett Kahr (Ed.). *New Horizons in Forensic Psychotherapy: Exploring the Work of Estela V. Welldon*, pp. 219-235. London: Karnac Books.

Dabbs, James McBride, and Dabbs, Mary Godwin (2000). *Heroes, Rogues, and Lovers: Testosterone and Behavior*. New York: McGraw-Hill / McGraw-Hill Companies.

Dabbs, James M., Jr., Frady, Robert L., Carr, Timothy S., and Besch,

Norma F. (1987). Saliva Testosterone and Criminal Violence in Young Adult Prison Inmates. *Psychosomatic Medicine*, 49, 174-182.

Darrow, Clarence (1922). *Crime: Its Cause and Treatment.* New York: Thomas Y. Crowell Company Publishers.

Daube, David (1947). *Studies in Biblical Law.* Cambridge: University Press / Cambridge University Press.

Davidson, James (2007). *The Greeks and Greek Love: A Radical Reappraisal of Homosexuality in Ancient Greece.* London: Weidenfeld and Nicolson.

Davies, Terence S. (1970). Cyproterone Acetate in Sexual Misbehaviour. *Medicine Science and the Law,* 10, 237.

Dawson, Jack (2016). My Experience as a Paedophile, Cured by NHS Psychoanalysis. StopSo [Specialist Treatment Organisation for Prevention of Sexual Offending]. [https://stopso.org.uk/my-experience-as-a-paedophile-cured-by-nhs-psychoanalysis/;Accessed on 16th March, 2019].

deMause, Lloyd (1974). The Evolution of Childhood. In Lloyd deMause (Ed.). *The History of Childhood,* pp. 1-73. New York: Psychohistory Press, Division of Atcom.

deMause, Lloyd (1988). On Writing Childhood History. *Journal of Psychohistory,* 16, 135-171.

deMause, Lloyd (1990). The History of Child Assault. *Journal of Psychohistory,* 18, 1-29.

deMause, Lloyd (1991). The Universality of Incest. *Journal of Psychohistory,* 19, 123-164.

deMause, Lloyd (2002). *The Emotional Life of Nations.* New York: Karnac / Other Press.

Dickens, Charles (1842). *American Notes for General Circulation: In Two Volumes. Vol. I.* London: Chapman and Hall.

Dickinson, Tommy (2015). *'Curing Queers': Mental Nurses and Their Patients, 1935-74.* Manchester: Manchester University Press.

Dicks, Henry V. (1972). *Licensed Mass Murder: A Socio-psychological Study of Some SS Killers.* London: Chatto Heinemann / Sussex University Press / Heinemann Educational Books.

Du Boys, Albert (1845). *Histoire du droit criminel des peuples anciens depuis la formation des sociétés jusqu'à l'établissement du Christianisme.* Paris: Joubert, Libraire de la Cour de Cassation.

Duckworth, Jeannie (2002). *Fagin's Children: Criminal Children in*

References

Victorian England. London: Hambledon and London.

East, William Norwood (1936). *Medical Aspects of Crime.* London: J. and A. Churchill.

Edwards, William D., Gabel, Wesley J., and Hosmer, Floyd E. (1986). On the Physical Death of Jesus Christ. *Journal of the American Medical Association.* 21st March, pp. 1455-1463.

Fallon, James (2013). *The Psychopath Inside: A Neuroscientist's Personal Journey into the Dark Side of the Brain.* New York: Current / Penguin Group, Penguin Group (USA), Penguin Random House Company.

Farber, Stephen, and Green, Marc (1993). *Hollywood on the Couch: A Candid Look at the Overheated Love Affair Between Psychiatrists and Moviemakers.* New York: William Morrow and Company.

Fazel, Seena, and Benning, Ram (2009). Suicide in Female Prisoners in England and Wales, 1978-2004. *British Journal of Psychiatry,* 194, 183-184.

Federn, Paul (1919). *Zur Psychologie der Revolution: Die vaterlose Gesellschaft. Nach Vorträgen in der Wiener psychoanalytischen Vereinigung und im Monistenbund.* Vienna: Anzengruber-Verlag Brüder Suschitzky.

Feld, Barry C., and Schaefer, Shelly (2010). The Right to Counsel in Juvenile Court: Law Reform to Deliver Legal Services and Reduce Justice by Geography. *Criminology and Public Policy,* 9, 327-356.

Ferenczi, Sándor (1919). Pszichoanalizis és kriminológia. In *A pszichoanalizis haladása: Ertekezések,* pp. 126-128. Budapest: Dick Manó Kiadása.

Ferenczi, Sándor (1922). *Populäre Vorträge über Psychoanalyse.* Vienna: Internationaler Psychoanalytischer Verlag.

Field, Leopold H. (1973). Benperidol in the Treatment of Sexual Offenders. *Medicine Science and the Law,* 13, 195-196.

Field, Leopold H., and Williams, Mark (1970). The Hormonal Treatment of Sexual Offenders. *Medicine Science and the Law,* 10, 27-34.

Field, Leopold H., and Williams, Mark (1971). A Note on the Scientific Assessment and Treatment of the Sexual Offender. *Medicine, Science and the Law,* 11, 180-181.

Ford, Richard (2018). Jail Staff Refer to Prisoners as Residents. *The Times.* 31st July, p. 4.

References

Freud, Sigmund (1886). "Bericht.": Ueber meine mit Universitäts-Jubiläums-Reisestipendium unternommene Reise nach Paris und Berlin. Oktober 1885 – Ende März 1886. In Josef Gicklhorn and Renée Gicklhorn (1960). *Sigmund Freuds akademische Laufbahn im Lichte der Dokumente*, pp. 82-89. Vienna: Verlag Urban und Schwarzenberg.

Freud, Sigmund (1895). Katharina .... In Josef Breuer and Sigmund Freud. *Studien über Hysterie*, pp. 106-116. Vienna: Franz Deuticke.

Freud, Sigmund (1896a). L'Hérédité et l'étiologie des névroses. *Revue Neurologique*, 4, 161-169.

Freud, Sigmund (1896b). Heredity and the Aetiology of the Neuroses. James Strachey (Transl.). In Sigmund Freud (1962). *The Standard Edition of the Complete Psychological Works of Sigmund Freud: Volume III. (1893-1899). Early Psycho-Analytic Publications*. James Strachey, Anna Freud, Alix Strachey, and Alan Tyson (Eds. and Transls.), pp. 143-156. London: Hogarth Press and the Institute of Psycho-Analysis.

Freud, Sigmund (1896c). Weitere Bemerkungen über die Abwehr-Neuropsychosen. *Neurologisches Centralblatt*, 15, 434-448.

Freud, Sigmund (1897a). Letter to Wilhelm Fliess. 28th April. In Sigmund Freud (1986). *Briefe an Wilhelm Fliess 1887-1904: Ungekürzte Ausgabe*. Jeffrey Moussaieff Masson and Michael Schröter (Eds.), pp. 250-252. Frankfurt am Main: S. Fischer / S. Fischer Verlag.

Freud, Sigmund (1897b). Letter to Wilhelm Fliess. 28th April. In Sigmund Freud (1985). *The Complete Letters of Sigmund Freud to Wilhelm Fliess: 1887-1904*. Jeffrey Moussaieff Masson (Ed.). Lottie Newman, Marianne Loring, and Jeffrey Moussaieff Masson (Transls.), pp. 236-238. Cambridge, Massachusetts: Belknap Press of Harvard University Press.

Freud, Sigmund (1900). *Die Traumdeutung*. Vienna: Franz Deuticke.

Freud, Sigmund (1905). *Drei Abhandlungen zur Sexualtheorie*. Vienna: Franz Deuticke.

Freud, Sigmund (1909). Analyse der Phobie eines 5jährigen Knaben. *Jahrbuch für psychoanalytische und psychopathologische Forschungen*, 1, 1-109.

Freud, Sigmund (1912a). Über einige Übereinstimmungen im

Seelenleben der Wilden und der Neurotiker: I. Die Inzest-
scheu. *Imago*, 1, 17-33.

Freud, Sigmund (1912b). Über einige Übereinstimmungen im
Seelenleben der Wilden und der Neurotiker: II. Das Tabu und
die Ambivalenz der Gefühlsregungen. *Imago*, 1, 213-227.

Freud, Sigmund (1912c). Über einige Übereinstimmungen im
Seelenleben der Wilden und der Neurotiker: II. Das Tabu und
die Ambivalenz der Gefühlsregungen. *Imago*, 1, 301-333.

Freud, Sigmund (1913a). *Totem und Tabu: Einige Übereinstimmungen im Seelenleben der Wilden und der Neurotiker.* Vienna: Hugo
Heller und Compagnie.

Freud, Sigmund (1913b). Über einige Übereinstimmungen im
Seelenleben der Wilden und der Neurotiker: III. Animismus,
Magie und Allmacht der Gedanken. *Imago*, 2, 1-21.

Freud, Sigmund (1913c). Über einige Übereinstimmungen im
Seelenleben der Wilden und der Neurotiker: IV. Die infantile
Wiederkehr des Totemismus. *Imago*, 2, 357-408.

Freud, Sigmund (1916). Einige Charaktertypen aus der psychoanalytischen Arbeit. *Imago*, 4, 317-336.

Freud, Sigmund (1925). Sigmund Freud. In Ludwig R. Grote
(Ed.). *Die Medizin der Gegenwart in Selbstdarstellungen*, pp.
1-52. Leipzig: Verlag von Felix Meiner.

Freud, Sigmund (1930). Letter to Marie Bonaparte. 20th February.
Box 137. Folder 7. Sigmund Freud Papers. Sigmund Freud
Collection. Manuscript Reading Room, Room 101, Manuscript
Division, James Madison Memorial Building, Library of Con-
gress, Washington, D.C., U.S.A.

Freud, Sigmund (1931a). Geleitworte: Prof. Dr. S. Freud, Wien. In
Georg Fuchs. *Wir Zuchthäusler: Erinnerungen des Zellengefangenen Nr. 2911*, pp. x-xi. Munich: Albert Langen.

Freud, Sigmund (1931b). Letter to Georg Fuchs. James Strachey
(Transl.). In Sigmund Freud (1964). *The Standard Edition
of the Complete Psychological Works of Sigmund Freud: Volume
XXII. (1932-36). New Introductory Lectures on Psycho-Analysis
and Other Works.* James Strachey, Anna Freud, Alix Strachey,
and Alan Tyson (Eds. and Transls.), pp. 251-252. London: Hogarth Press and the Institute of Psycho-Analysis.

Freud, Sigmund (1933). Letter to Grace Pailthorpe. 8th November. Box 38. Folder 10. Sigmund Freud Papers. Sigmund
Freud Collection. Manuscript Reading Room, Room 101,

References

Manuscript Division, James Madison Memorial Building, Library of Congress, Washington, D.C., U.S.A.

Freud, Sigmund (1992). *The Diary of Sigmund Freud: 1929-1939. A Record of the Final Decade.* Michael Molnar (Ed. and Transl.). London: Hogarth Press.

Fuchs, Georg (1931). *Wir Zuchthäusler: Erinnerungen des Zellengefangenen Nr. 2911.* Munich: Albert Langen.

Gallo, Rubén (2012). A Wild Freudian in Mexico: Raúl Carrancá y Trujillo. *Psychoanalysis and History,* 14, 253-268.

Gardner, George E. (1972). William Healy: 1869-1963. *Journal of the American Academy of Child Psychiatry,* 11, 1-29.

Gardner, George E. (1978). William Healy: 1869-1963. In George E. Gifford, Jr. (Ed.). *Psychoanalysis, Psychotherapy, and the New England Medical Scene, 1894-1944,* pp. 251-272. New York: Science History Publications / USA, Neale Watson Academic Publications.

Geary, Laurence M. (1990). O'Connorite Bedlam: Feargus and His Grand-Nephew, Arthur. *Medical History,* 34, 125-143.

Gelder, Michael; Gath, Dennis, and Mayou, Richard (1983). *Oxford Textbook of Psychiatry.* Oxford: Oxford University Press.

Gibb, Frances (2016). Sex Cases Take Up Half of Court Time. *The Times.* 7th May, p. 14.

Gilligan, James (1996). *Violence: Our Deadly Epidemic and Its Causes.* New York: G.P. Putnam's Sons.

Gilligan, James (2001). *Preventing Violence.* London: Thames and Hudson.

Gilligan, James (2016). Can Psychoanalysis Help Us to Understand the Causes and Prevention of Violence? *Psychoanalytic Psychotherapy,* 30, 125-137.

Glasser, Mervin (1979). Some Aspects of the Role of Aggression in the Perversions. In Ismond Rosen (Ed.). *Sexual Deviation: Second Edition,* pp. 278-305. Oxford: Oxford University Press.

Glasser, Mervin (1988). Psychodynamic Aspects of Paedophilia. *Psychoanalytic Psychotherapy,* 3, 121-135.

Glasser, Mervin (1990). Paedophilia. In Robert Bluglass and Paul Bowden (Eds.). *Principles and Practice of Forensic Psychiatry,* pp. 739-748. Edinburgh: Churchill Livingstone / Medical Division of Longman Group UK.

Glover, Edward (1932). The Psychology of Crime: V. *British Journal of Medical Psychology,* 12, 270-272.

Glover, Edward (1933). The Relation of Perversion-Formation to the Development of Reality-Sense. *International Journal of Psycho-Analysis*, 14, 486-504.

Glover, Edward (1936). *The Dangers of Being Human.* London: George Allen and Unwin.

Glover, Edward (1956). Psycho-Analysis and Criminology: A Political Survey. *International Journal of Psycho-Analysis*, 37, 311-317.

Glover, Edward (1960). *Selected Papers on Psycho-Analysis: Volume II. The Roots of Crime.* London: Imago Publishing Company.

Glover, Edward (1961). Foreword. In Elizabeth Orman Tuttle. *The Crusade Against Capital Punishment in Great Britain*, pp. ix-x. London: Stevens and Sons, and Chicago, Illinois: Quadrangle Books.

Glover, Edward (1964). Aggression and Sado-Masochism. In Ismond Rosen (Ed.). *The Pathology and Treatment of Sexual Deviation: A Methodological Approach*, pp. 146-163. London: Oxford University Press.

Golden, Charles J., Jackson, Michele L., Peterson-Rohne, Angela, and Gontkovsky, Samuel T. (1996). Neuropsychological Correlates of Violence and Aggression: A Review of the Clinical Literature. *Aggression and Violent Behavior*, 1, 3-25.

Grafman, Jordan; Schwab, Karen; Pridgen, Anthony, and Salazar, Andres M. (1995). Do Frontal Lobe Lesions Lead to a Greater Likelihood of Aggression and Violence? *Neurology*, 45, Supplement 4, A389.

Grafman, Jordan; Schwab, Karen; Warden, Deborah; Pridgen, Anthony; Brown, Herbert R., and Salazar, Andres M. (1996). A Report of the Vietnam Head Injury Study. *Neurology*, 46, 1231-1238.

Gray, John P. (1857). Homicide in Insanity. *American Journal of Insanity*, 14, 119-145.

Grünhut, Max (1941). John Howard. *Howard Journal*, 6, 34-44.

Guelzo, Allen C. (2013). *Gettysburg: The Last Invasion.* New York: Alfred A. Knopf.

Guttmacher, Manfred S., and Weihofen, Henry (1952). *Psychiatry and the Law.* New York: W.W. Norton and Company.

Hackett, Simon; Masson, Helen; Balfe, Myles, and Phillips, Josie (2013). Individual, Family and Abuse Characteristics of 700 British Child and Adolescent Sexual Abusers. *Child Abuse Review*, 22, 232-245.

References

Hakeem, Az (2009). 'Forensic Group Psychotherapy': Estela Well-don's Contribution to Working with Groups at the Portman Clinic. *British Journal of Psychotherapy*, 25, 230-238.

Hammer, Emanuel F., and Glueck, Bernard C., Jr. (1955). Psycho-dynamic Patterns in the Sex Offender: I: Fear of the Adult Female Sex Object and Feelings of Genital Inadequacy. In Paul H. Hoch and Joseph Zubin (Eds.). *Psychiatry and the Law: The Proceedings of the Forty-Third Annual Meeting of the American Psychopathological Association, Held in New York City, June, 1953*, pp. 157-168. New York: Grune and Stratton.

Happel, Clara (1925). Aus der Analyse eines Falles von Päderastie: Vortrag aus der I. Deutschen Psychoanalytischen Zusammen-kunft in Würzburg, Oktober 1924. *Internationale Zeitschrift für Psychoanalyse*, 11, 206-211.

Harper, Robert Francis (Transl.). (1904). *The Code of Hammurabi: King of Babylon. About 2250 B.C. Autographed Text. Translit-eration. Translation. Glossary. Index of Subjects. Lists of Proper Names. Signs. Numerals. Corrections and Erasures with Map. Frontispiece and Photograph of Text.* Chicago, Illinois: University of Chicago Press / Callaghan and Company, and London: Luzac and Company.

Harrison, Marissa A., Murphy, Erin A., Ho, Lavina Y., Bowers, Thomas G., and Flaherty, Claire V. (2015). Female Serial Kill-ers in the United States: Means, Motives, and Makings. *Journal of Forensic Psychiatry and Psychology*, 26, 383-406.

Hartnack, Christiane (2001). *Psychoanalysis in Colonial India.* New Delhi: Oxford University Press.

Haycock, Dean A. (2014). *Murderous Minds: Exploring the Crimi-nal Psychopathic Brain: Neurological Imaging and the Manifesta-tion of Evil.* New York: Pegasus Books.

Healy, William (1915). *The Individual Delinquent: A Text-Book of Diagnosis and Prognosis for All Concerned in Understanding Offenders.* Boston, Massachusetts: Little, Brown, and Company.

Healy, William, and Bronner, Augusta F. (1922). *Judge Baker Foun-dation: Case Studies. Series I. Case 1.* Boston, Massachusetts: Judge Baker Foundation.

Healy, William, and Bronner, Augusta F. (1926). *Delinquents and Criminals: Their Making and Unmaking. Studies in Two Ameri-can Cities.* New York: Macmillan Company.

Herrmann, Werner M., and Beach. R.C. (1980). Pharmacotherapy for Sexual Offenders: Review of the Action of Antiandrogens with Special Reference to Their Psychic Effects. In Thomas A. Ban and Fritz A. Freyhan (Eds.). *Drug Treatment of Sexual Dysfunction*, pp. 182-194. Berlin: S. Karger.

Hill, Simon A., Mitchell, Paul, and Leipold, Alexandra (2017). Transfers of Mentally Disordered Adolescents from Custodial Settings to Psychiatric Hospital in England and Wales 2004-2014. *Journal of Forensic Psychiatry and Psychology*, 28, 1-9.

Hitler, Adolf (1927 [1926]). Zweiter Band: Die nationalſozial-iſtiſche Bewegung. In Adolf Hitler (1930). *Mein Kampf: Zwei Bände in einem Band. Ungekürzte Ausgabe. Erster Band: Eine Abrechnung. Zweiter Band: Die nationalſozialiſtiſche Bewegung. IV. Auflage*, pp. 407-781. Munich: Verlag Franz Eher Nachfol-ger.

Hopper, Earl (1991). Encapsulation as a Defence Against the Fear of Annihilation. *International Journal of Psycho-Analysis*, 72, 607-624.

Hopper, Earl (1995). A Psychoanalytical Theory of 'Drug Addiction': Unconscious Fantasies of Homosexuality, Compulsions and Masturbation within the Context of Traumatogenic Processes. *International Journal of Psycho-Analysis*, 76, 1121-1142.

Howard, Derek L. (1958). *John Howard: Prison Reformer*. London: Christopher Johnson.

Hurry, Anne (1990). Bisexual Conflict and Paedophilic Fantasies in the Analysis of a Late Adolescent. *Journal of Child Psychotherapy*, 16, 5-28.

Hutchinson, Robert (2006). *Elizabeth's Spy Master: Francis Walsingham and the Secret War That Saved England*. London: Weidenfeld and Nicolson / Orion Publishing Group.

Huttunen, Matti O., and Niskanen, Pekka (1978). Prenatal Loss of Father and Psychiatric Disorders. *Archives of General Psychiatry*, 35, 429-431.

Institute Board Meetings: 16.1.1925 to 30.4.1945 (1925-1945). Archives of the British Psychoanalytical Society, British Psychoanalytical Society, Byron House, Maida Vale, London.

Israel, James (1880). Ein Beitrag zur Würdigung des Werthes der Castration bei hysterischen Frauen: (Vortrag, gehalten in der Berliner medicinischen Gesellschaft am 14. Januar 1880). *Berliner Klinische Wochenschrift*. 26th April, pp. 242-245.

Johns, Claude H.W. (1914). *The Relations Between the Laws of Bab-

ylonia and the Laws of the Hebrew Peoples: The Scheich Lectures. 1912. London: Humphrey Milford / Oxford University Press.

Jones, Ernest (1953). *The Life and Work of Sigmund Freud: Volume 1. The Formative Years and the Great Discoveries. 1856-1900.* New York: Basic Books.

Jones, Ernest (1957). *The Life and Work of Sigmund Freud: Volume 3. The Last Phase. 1919-1939.* New York: Basic Books.

JUST 1/802 (Staffs. 1272), m. 46 dorse (n.d.). Cited in Zefira Entin Rokeah (1990). Unnatural Child Death Among Christians and Jews in Medieval England. *Journal of Psychohistory*, 18, 181-226.

Kahr, Brett (1991). The Sexual Molestation of Children: Historical Perspectives. *Journal of Psychohistory*, 19, 191-214.

Kahr, Brett (1996a). *D.W. Winnicott: A Biographical Portrait.* London: H. Karnac (Books).

Kahr, Brett (1996b). Donald Winnicott and the Foundations of Child Psychotherapy. *Journal of Child Psychotherapy*, 22, 327-342.

Kahr, Brett (Ed.). (2001a). *Forensic Psychotherapy and Psychopathology: Winnicottian Perspectives.* London: H. Karnac (Books).

Kahr, Brett (2001b). Winnicott's Contribution to the Study of Dangerousness. In Brett Kahr (Ed.). *Forensic Psychotherapy and Psychopathology: Winnicottian Perspectives*, pp. 1-10. London: H. Karnac (Books).

Kahr, Brett (2004). Juvenile Paedophilia: The Psychodynamics of an Adolescent. In Charles W. Socarides and Loretta R. Loeb (Eds.). *The Mind of the Paedophile: Psychoanalytic Perspectives*, pp. 95-119. London: H. Karnac (Books).

Kahr, Brett (2007). *Sex and the Psyche.* London: Allen Lane / Penguin Books, Penguin Group.

Kahr, Brett (2008). *Who's Been Sleeping in Your Head?: The Secret World of Sexual Fantasies.* New York: Basic Books / Perseus Books Group.

Kahr, Brett (2010). Four Unknown Freud Anecdotes. *American Imago*, 67, 301-312.

Kahr, Brett (2012). Foreword. In Andrew Balfour, Mary Morgan, and Christopher Vincent (Eds.). *How Couple Relationships Shape Our World: Clinical Practice, Research, and Policy Perspectives*, pp. xvii-xxi. London: Karnac Books.

Kahr, Brett (2014a). Series Editor's Foreword: Towards Forensic Disability Psychotherapy. In Alan Corbett. *Disabling Perversions: Forensic Psychotherapy with People with Intellectual Disabilities*, pp. xiii-xxii. London: Karnac Books.

Kahr, Brett (2014b). *"smyten wt a ffransy": King Henry VI and Medieval Madness*. Unpublished Typescript.

Kahr, Brett (2016). Series Editor's Foreword. In Barry Maletzky. *Sexual Abuse and the Sexual Offender: Common Man or Monster?*, pp. xi-xiv. London: Karnac Books.

Kahr, Brett (Ed.). (2018a). *New Horizons in Forensic Psychotherapy: Exploring the Work of Estela V. Welldon*. London: Karnac Books.

Kahr, Brett (2018b). Estela at La Scala. In Brett Kahr (Ed.). *New Horizons in Forensic Psychotherapy: Exploring the Work of Estela V. Welldon*, pp. 1-14. London: Karnac Books.

Kahr, Brett (2018c). "No Intolerable Persons" or "Lewd Pregnant Women": Towards a History of Forensic Psychoanalysis. In Brett Kahr (Ed.). *New Horizons in Forensic Psychotherapy: Exploring the Work of Estela V. Welldon*, pp. 17-87. London: Karnac Books.

Kahr, Brett (2018d). Committing Crimes without Breaking the Law: Unconscious Sadism in the "Non-Forensic" Patient. In Brett Kahr (Ed.). *New Horizons in Forensic Psychotherapy: Exploring the Work of Estela V. Welldon*, pp. 239-261. London: Karnac Books.

Kahr, Brett (2018e). Sigmund Freud's Revolution in Psychiatry. *Friends News. Freud Museum London*, pp. 14-16.

Kahr, Brett (2019). Foreword. In Andrew Balfour, Christopher Clulow, and Kate Thompson (Eds.). *Engaging Couples: New Directions in Therapeutic Work with Families*, pp. xv-xvii. London: Routledge / Taylor and Francis Group, and Abingdon, Oxfordshire: Routledge / Taylor and Francis Group.

Kahr, Brett (2020). *Bombs in the Consulting Room: Surviving Psychological Shrapnel*. London: Routledge / Taylor and Francis Group, and Abingdon, Oxfordshire: Routledge / Taylor and Francis Group.

Karpman, Ben (1950). A Case of Paedophilia (Legally Rape) Cured by Psychoanalysis. *Psychoanalytic Review*, 37, 235-276.

Kempf-Leonard, Kimberly (2010). Does Having an Attorney Provide a Better Outcome?: The Right to Counsel Does Not Mean Attorneys Help Youths. *Criminology and Public Policy*, 9, 357-363.

Kirtchuk, Gabriel; Gordon, John; Doctor, Ronald, and Ingram, Richard (2016). A Fertile Matrix: The Birth of the Forensic Psychotherapy Society. *Psychoanalytic Psychotherapy*, 3, 182-195.

Klein, Melanie (1932a). *Die Psychoanalyse des Kindes*. Vienna: Internationaler Psychoanalytischer Verlag.

Klein, Melanie (1932b). *The Psycho-Analysis of Children*. Alix Strachey (Transl.). London: Hogarth Press and the Institute of Psycho-Analysis.

Kraepelin, Emil (1913). *Psychiatrie: Ein Lehrbuch für Studierende und Ärzte. Achte, vollständig umgearbeitete Auflage. III. Band. Klinische Psychiatrie. II. Teil*. Leipzig: Verlag von Johann Ambrosius Barth.

Kraepelin, Emil (1918a). *Hundert Jahre Psychiatrie: Ein Beitrag zur Geschichte menschlicher Gesittung*. Berlin: Verlag von Julius Springer.

Kraepelin, Emil (1918b). Hundert Jahre Psychiatrie. *Zeitschrift für die gesamte Neurologie und Psychiatrie*, 38, 161-275.

Lake, Peter, and Questier, Michael (2011). *The Trials of Margaret Clitherow: Persecution, Martyrdom and the Politics of Sanctity in Elizabethan England*. London: Continuum / Continuum International Publishing Group.

Lange, Johannes (1929). *Verbrechen als Schicksal: Studien an kriminellen Zwillingen*. Leipzig: Georg Thieme, Verlag.

Langlands, Rebecca (2006). *Sexual Morality in Ancient Rome*. Cambridge: Cambridge University Press.

Lanyado, Monica; Hodges, Jill; Bentovim, Arnon; Andreou, Chriso, and Williams, Bryn (1995). Understanding Boys Who Sexually Abuse Other Children: A Clinical Illustration. *Psychoanalytic Psychotherapy*, 9, 231-242.

Large, David Clay (2015). *The Grand Spas of Central Europe: A History of Intrigue, Politics, Art, and Healing*. Lanham, Maryland: Rowman and Littlefield / Rowman and Littlefield Publishing Group.

Lazar-Geroe, Clara (1942). First Annual Report of the Melbourne Institute for Psychoanalysis for the Year 1941, pp. 613-615. In Notes. *Psychoanalytic Quarterly*, 11, 611-617.

Lear, Andrew (2008). Courtship. In Andrew Lear and Eva Cantarella. *Images of Ancient Greek Pederasty: Boys Were Their Gods*, pp. 38-62. London: Routledge / Taylor and Francis Group, and

Abingdon, Oxfordshire: Routledge / Taylor and Francis Group.

Lecky, William Edward Hartpole (1869). *History of European Morals from Augustus to Charlemagne: In Two Volumes. Vol. I.* London: Longmans, Green, and Company.

Levy, John (1932). A Mental Hygiene Study of Juvenile Delinquency: Its Causes and Treatment. *American Journal of Psychiatry*, 12, 73-142.

Lewis, Dorothy Otnow (1998). *Guilty by Reason of Insanity: A Psychiatrist Explores the Minds of Killers.* New York: Fawcett Columbine / Ballantine Publishing Group, Random House.

Lewis, Dorothy Otnow; Pincus, Jonathan H., Bard, Barbara; Richardson, Ellis; Prichep, Leslie S., Feldman, Marilyn, and Yeager, Catherine (1988). Neuropsychiatric, Psychoeducational, and Family Characteristics of 14 Juveniles Condemned to Death in the United States. *American Journal of Psychiatry*, 145, 584-589.

Lewis, Dorothy Otnow; Yeager, Catherine A., Swica, Yael; Pincus, Jonathan H., and Lewis, Melvin (1997). Objective Documentation of Child Abuse and Dissociation in 12 Murderers with Dissociative Identity Disorder. *American Journal of Psychiatry*, 154, 1703-1710.

Lincoln, Abraham (1863). Letter to John P. Gray. 10th September, pp. 286-287. In Anonymous (1864). The Case of Dr. David M. Wright: For the Murder of Lieutenant Sanborn – Plea, Insanity. *American Journal of Insanity*, 20, 284-300.

Lombroso, Cesare (1876). *L'Uomo delinquente: Studiato in rapporto alla antropologia, alla medicina legale ed alle discipline carcerarie.* Milan: Ulrico Hoepli, Libraio-Editore.

Lowndes, Frederick W. (1887). Venereal Diseases in Girls of Tender Age. *The Lancet.* 22nd January, pp. 168-169.

Luntz, Barbara K., and Widom, Cathy Spatz (1994). Antisocial Personality Disorder in Abused and Neglected Children Grown Up. *American Journal of Psychiatry*, 151, 670-674.

Lyons, Lewis (2003). *The History of Punishment.* London: Amber Books.

Mackwood, John C. (1947). Discussion on the Social Aspects of Homosexuality. *Proceedings of the Royal Society of Medicine, Section of Psychiatry*, 40, 591-592.

Mackwood, John C. (1949). The Psychological Treatment of Offenders in Prison. *British Journal of Psychology: General Section*, 40, 5-22.

Mackwood, John C. (1954). Psychotherapy in Prisons and Corrective Institutions: [Abridged]. *Proceedings of the Royal Society of Medicine, Section of Psychiatry*, 47, 220-221.

Maimonides (c. 1170-c. 1180). *The Code of Maimonides: Book Fourteen. The Book of Judges*. Abraham M. Hershman (Transl.). (1949). New Haven, Connecticut: Yale University Press, and London: Geoffrey Cumberlege / Oxford University Press.

Mandeville, Bernard (1725). *An Enquiry into the Causes of the Frequent Executions at Tyburn: And A Proposal for ſome Regulations concerning Felons in Prison, and the good Effects to be Expected from them. To which is Added, A Diſcourſe on Transportation, and a Method to render that Puniſhment more Effectual*. London: J. Roberts.

Marks, Alfred (n.d. [1908]). *Tyburn Tree: Its History and Annals*. London: Brown, Langham and Company.

Martial [Marcus Valerius Martialis] (1973). *The Epigrams of Martial*. James Michie (Transl.). London: Hart-Davis, MacGibbon.

Martialis, Marcus Valerius (1773). *Epigrammata: In Uſum Scholae Westmonasteriensis. Editio Quarta. Auctior & Emendator*. London: W. Ginger.

Marzano, Lisa; Fazel, Seena; Rivlin, Adrienne, and Hawton, Keith (2010). Psychiatric Disorders in Women Prisoners Who Have Engaged in Near-Lethal Self-Harm: Case-Control Study. *British Journal of Psychiatry*, 197, 219-226.

Maslen, Matthew W., and Mitchell, Piers D. (2006). Medical Theories on the Cause of Death in Crucifixion. *Journal of the Royal Society of Medicine*, 99, 185-188.

Masson, Jeffrey Moussaieff (1984). *The Assault on Truth: Freud's Suppression of the Seduction Theory*. New York: Farrar, Straus and Giroux.

Masters, Brian (1985). *Killing for Company: The Case of Dennis Nilsen*. London: Jonathan Cape.

Masters, Brian (1993). *The Shrine of Jeffrey Dahmer*. London: Hodder and Stoughton, and Dunton Green, Sevenoaks, Kent: Hodder and Stoughton, Hodder and Stoughton Limited.

McKenzie, Andrea (2007). *Tyburn's Martyrs: Execution in England, 1675-1775*. London: Hambledon Continuum / Continuum Books, Continuum UK.

Memorandum Submitted by the Institute of Psycho-Analysis to the Royal Commission on Capital Punishment (1950). G10/BA/

References

F01/09. Archives of the British Psychoanalytical Society, British Psychoanalytical Society, Byron House, Maida Vale, London.

Menninger, Karl (1968). *The Crime of Punishment*. New York: Viking Press.

Merloni, Raffaele (1933). Psicoanalisi e criminalità. *Rivista Italiana di Psicoanalisi*, 2, 355-371.

Mezey, Gillian; Vizard, Eileen; Hawkes, Colin, and Austin, Richard (1991). A Community Treatment Programme for Convicted Child Sex Offenders: A Preliminary Report. *Journal of Forensic Psychiatry*, 2, 11-25.

Minne, Carine, and Kassman, Paul (2018). Working with Gangs and within Gang Culture: A Pilot for Changing the Game. In Brett Kahr (Ed.). *New Horizons in Forensic Psychotherapy: Exploring the Work of Estela V. Welldon*, pp. 183-201. London: Karnac Books.

Mohr, George J. (1966). August Aichhorn: 1878-1949. Friend of the Wayward Youth. In Franz Alexander, Samuel Eisenstein, and Martin Grotjahn (Eds.). *Psychoanalytic Pioneers*, pp. 348-359. New York: Basic Books.

Motz, Anna (2008). Women Who Kill: When Fantasy Becomes Reality. In Ronald Doctor (Ed.). *Murder: A Psychotherapeutic Investigation*, pp. 51-64. London: Karnac Books.

Motz, Anna (2009). Thinking the Unthinkable: Facing Maternal Abuse. *British Journal of Psychotherapy*, 25, 203-213.

Mullins, Claud (1943). "Can Delinquency Be Scientifically Treated?" *Howard Journal*, 6, 141-144.

Mush, John (1849). *Life and Death of Margaret Clitherow, The Martyr of York*. William Nicholson (Ed.). London: Richardson and Son.

Naphy, William (2002). *Sex Crimes: From Renaissance to Enlightenment*. Brimscombe Port, Stroud, Gloucestershire: Tempus / Tempus Publishing.

National Children's Home (1992). *Children Who Abuse Other Children*. London: National Children's Home.

Natterson, Joseph M. (1966). Theodor Reik: b. 1888. Masochism in Modern Man. In Franz Alexander, Samuel Eisenstein, and Martin Grotjahn (Eds.). *Psychoanalytic Pioneers*, pp. 249-264. New York: Basic Books.

Newth, Alfred H. (1884). The Value of Electricity in the Treatment of Insanity. *Journal of Mental Science*, 30, 354-359.

References

Niehoff, Debra (1999). *The Biology of Violence: How Understanding the Brain, Behavior, and Environment Can Break the Vicious Circle of Aggression.* New York: Free Press / Simon and Schuster.

Orrells, Daniel (2015). *Sex: Antiquity and its Legacy.* London: I.B. Tauris and Company.

Overholser, Winfred (1952). Vernon C. Branham, M.D.: 1889-1951. *American Journal of Psychiatry*, 108, 640.

Paget, Walburga (1923). *Embassies of Other Days: And Further Recollections. Volume II.* London: Hutchinson and Company.

Pailthorpe, Grace W. (1932). *Studies in the Psychology of Delinquency.* London: His Majesty's Stationery Office.

Patterson, Gerard A. (1997). *Debris of Battle: The Wounded of Gettysburg.* Mechanicsburg, Pennsylvania: Stackpole Books.

Pincus, Jonathan H. (2001). *Base Instincts: What Makes Killers Kill?* New York: W.W. Norton and Company.

Plutarch (n.d.). *Plutarch's Lives: The Translation Called Dryden's. In Five Volumes. Volume the First.* Arthur H. Clough (Transl.). (1893). London: John C. Nimmo.

Plvtarchi [Plutarch] (n.d.). *Vitarvm Parallelarvm: Volvmen Primvm, Thesevm, Romvlvm, Lycvrgvm, Nvmam, Solonem, Poplicolam, Themistoclem, Camillvm, Periclem, Fabivm Maximvm Tenens.* Ionnes Iacobvs Reiske [Johann Jakob Reiske] (Ed.). (1774). Leipzig: Gotth. Theoph. Georgi.

Podolsky, Edward (1956). Notes on Motiveless Murder. *International Journal of Social Psychiatry*, 1, Number 4, 42-45.

Powell, Claire; Ciclitira, Karen, and Marzano, Lisa (2017). Mother-Infant Separations in Prison: A Systematic Attachment-Focused Review of the Academic and Grey Literature. *Journal of Forensic Psychiatry and Psychology*, 28, 790-810.

Powell, Claire; Marzano, Lisa, and Ciclitira, Karen (2017). Mother-Infant Separations in Prison: A Systematic Attachment-Focused Policy Review. *Journal of Forensic Psychiatry and Psychology*, 28, 274-289.

Power, Denis J. (1976). Sexual Deviation and Crime. *Medicine, Science and the Law*, 16, 111-128.

Power, Denis J., and Selwood, D.H.D. (1987). *Criminal Law and Psychiatry.* n.p.: Barry Rose Books / Kluwer Law Publishers.

Preventing Suicide in Community and Custodial Settings: NICE Guideline (2018). National Institute for Health and Care Excellence. London: National Institute for Health and Care

Excellence, Public Health England. [https://www.nice.org.uk/guidance/ng105/resources/preventing-suicide-in-community-and-custodial-settings-pdf-66141539632069; Accessed on 9th March, 2019].

Prichard, James Cowles (1822). *A Treatise on Diseases of the Nervous System: Part the First: Comprising Convulsive and Maniacal Affections.* London: Thomas and George Underwood.

Prichard, James Cowles (1835). *A Treatise on Insanity and Other Disorders Affecting the Mind.* London: Sherwood, Gilbert, and Piper.

Prichard, James Cowles (1842). *On the Different Forms of Insanity, in Relation to Jurisprudence, Designed for the Use of Persons Concerned in Legal Questions Regarding Unsoundness of Mind.* London: Hippolyte Baillière, Publisher, and Paris: J.B. Baillière.

Priestley, Joseph C., Fry, Theodore W., Kelly, Elizabeth H., Martineau, Clara; Norris, Arthur, H., Parr, Robert J., Rackham, Clara D., and Stephenson, Guy (1925). *Report of the Departmental Committee on Sexual Offences Against Young Persons: Presented to Parliament by Command of His Majesty.* London: His Majesty's Stationery Office.

Prior, Pauline M. (2003). Dangerous Lunacy: The Misuse of Mental Health Law in Nineteenth-Century Ireland. *Journal of Forensic Psychiatry and Psychology,* 14, 525-541.

Puri, Basant K., Baxter, Richard, and Cordess, Christopher C. (1995). Characteristics of Fire-Setters: A Study and Proposed Multiaxial Psychiatric Classification. *British Journal of Psychiatry,* 166, 393-396.

Qvarsell, Roger (1993). Forensic Psychiatry, Criminology and Criminal Law in Sweden During the 20th Century. In Leonie de Goei and Joost Vijselaar (Eds.). *Proceedings of the 1st European Congress on the History of Psychiatry and Mental Health Care: 's-Hertogenbosch, The Netherlands, 24-26 October, 1990,* pp. 263-266. Rotterdam: Erasmus Publishing, and Utrecht: Netherlands Institute of Mental Health.

Radzinowicz, Leon (1978). John Howard. In John C. Freeman (Ed.). *Prisons Past and Future,* pp. 7-13. London: Heinemann / Heinemann Educational Books.

Rafter, Nicole (2008). *The Criminal Brain: Understanding Biological Theories of Crime.* New York: New York University Press.

Raine, Adrian (2013). *The Anatomy of Violence: The Biological Roots of Crime*. New York: Pantheon Books / Random House.

Raine, Adrian; Buchsbaum, Monte, and LaCasse, Lori (1997). Brain Abnormalities in Murderers Indicated by Positron Emission Tomography. *Biological Psychiatry*, 42, 495-508.

Raine, Adrian; Buchsbaum, Monte S., Stanley, Jill; Lottenberg, Steven; Abel, Leonard, and Stoddard, Jacqueline (1994). Selective Reductions in Prefrontal Glucose Metabolism in Murderers. *Biological Psychiatry*, 36, 365-373.

Raine, Adrian; Lencz, Todd; Bihrle, Susan; LaCasse, Lori, and Colletti, Patrick (2000). Reduced Prefrontal Gray Matter Volume and Reduced Autonomic Activity in Antisocial Personality Disorder. *Archives of General Psychiatry*, 57, 119-127.

Rank, Otto (Ed.). (1907a). Vortragsabend: Am 23. Januar 1907. In Herman Nunberg and Ernst Federn (Eds.). (1976). *Protokolle der Wiener Psychoanalytischen Vereinigung: Band I. 1906-1908*, pp. 77-86. Frankfurt am Main: S. Fischer / S. Fischer Verlag.

Rank, Otto (Ed.). (1907b). Vortragsabend: Am 6. Februar 1907. In Herman Nunberg and Ernst Federn (Eds.). (1976). *Protokolle der Wiener Psychoanalytischen Vereinigung: Band I. 1906-1908*, pp. 97-104. Frankfurt am Main: S. Fischer / S. Fischer Verlag.

Rank, Otto (Ed.). (1907c). Scientific Meeting on February 6, 1907. In Herman Nunberg and Ernst Federn (Eds.). (1962). *Minutes of the Vienna Psychoanalytic Society: Volume I: 1906-1908*. Margarethe Nunberg (Transl.), pp. 103-110. New York: International Universities Press.

Rank, Otto (Ed.). (1907d). Vortragsabend: Am 10. April 1907. In Herman Nunberg and Ernst Federn (Eds.). (1976). *Protokolle der Wiener Psychoanalytischen Vereinigung: Band I. 1906-1908*, pp. 150-156. Frankfurt am Main: S. Fischer / S. Fischer Verlag.

Ransom, Janet (2018). Young Rikers Inmates Say They Were Shipped Upstate, Held in Isolation and Beaten. *New York Times*. 29th December, p. A19.

Ray, Isaac (1866). The Insanity of Women Produced by Desertion or Seduction. *American Journal of Insanity*, 23, 263-274.

Read, Conyers (1925). *Mr Secretary Walsingham and the Policy of Queen Elizabeth: Vol. II*. Oxford: Clarendon Press, and London: Oxford University Press.

Richardson, William (2004). Topcliffe, Richard (1531-1604).

References

In H. Colin G. Matthew and Brian Harrison (Eds.). *Oxford Dictionary of National Biography: In Association with the British Academy. From the Earliest Times to the Year 2000. Volume 55. Tonson-Usher*, pp. 28-30. Oxford: Oxford University Press.

Ritschel, Nelson O'Ceallaigh (2017). *Bernard Shaw, W.T. Stead, and the New Journalism: Whitechapel, Parnell, Titanic, and the Great War.* Cham: Palgrave Macmillan / Springer Nature, Springer International Publishing.

Rivlin, Adrienne; Hawton, Keith; Marzano, Lisa, and Fazel, Seena (2010). Psychiatric Disorders in Male Prisoners Who Made Near-Lethal Suicide Attempts: Case-Control Study. *British Journal of Psychiatry*, 197, 313-319.

Roth, Alisa (2018). *Insane: America's Criminal Treatment of Mental Illness.* New York: Basic Books / Hachette Book Group.

Rumbelow, Donald (1982). *The Triple Tree: Newgate, Tyburn and Old Bailey.* London: Harrap.

Rumney, David (1992). Origin and Early Struggles. In Eve Saville and David Rumney. *'Let Justice Be Done!': Your National and International Crime Forum After its Diamond Jubilee Year. A History of the I.S.T.D. A Study of Crime and Delinquency from 1931 to 1992*, pp. 1-9. London: Institute for the Study and Treatment of Delinquency.

Rymer, Thoma [Thomas Rymer] (Ed.). (1741). *Foedera, Conventiones, Literae, et cujuſcunque generis Acta Publica, inter Reges Angliae, et alios quoſvis Imperatores, Reges, Pontifices, Principes, vel Communitates, ab Inuente Saeculo duodecimo, viz. ab Anno 1101: Ad noſtra uſque tempora, habita aut tractata. Ex Autographis, infra Secretiores Archivorum Regiorum Theſaurarias per multa Saecula reconditis, fideliter exſcripta. In lucem missa de mandato nuperae Reginae. Editio Tertia, Ad originales Chartas in Turri Londinenſi denuo ſumma fide collata et emendata, ſtudio Georgii Holmes. Tomi Quinti Pars I. et II.* The Hague: Joannem Neaulme.

Schreiber, Flora Rheta (1973). *Sybil.* Chicago, Illinois: Henry Regnery Company.

Schreiber, Flora Rheta (1983). *The Shoemaker: The Anatomy of a Psychotic.* New York: Simon and Schuster.

Schults, Raymond L. (1972). *Crusader in Babylon: W.T. Stead and the Pall Mall Gazette.* Lincoln, Nebraska: University of Nebraska Press.

Schwartz, Robert G., and Levick, Marsha (2010). When a "Right" is Not Enough: Implementation of the Right to Counsel in an Age of Ambivalence. *Criminology and Public Policy*, 9, 365-373.

Scott, Peter D. (1964). Definition, Classification, Prognosis and Treatment. In Ismond Rosen (Ed.). *The Pathology and Treatment of Sexual Deviation: A Methodological Approach*, pp. 87-119. London: Oxford University Press.

Seneca, Lucius Annaeus (n.d. [a] [c. 40s CE]). De Ira: Ad Novatum. In L. Annaei Senecae [Lucius Annaeus Seneca] (1797). *Opera Omnia: Qvae Svpersvnt. Volvmen Primvm*. Fridericvs Ernestvs Rvhkopf [Friedrich Ernst Ruhkopf] (Transl.), pp. 1-154. Leipzig: Libraria Weidmannia.

Seneca, Lucius Annaeus (n.d. [b] [c. 40s C.E.]). On Anger: Book 3. To Novatus. In Lucius Annaeus Seneca (2007). *Dialogues and Essays*. John Davie (Transl.), pp. 18-52. Oxford: Oxford University Press.

Seruca, Tânia, and Silva, Carlos F. (2015). Recidivist Criminal Behaviour and Executive Functions: A Comparative Study. *Journal of Forensic Psychiatry and Psychology*, 26, 699-717.

Shea, Steven J. (1993). Personality Characteristics of Self-Mutilating Male Prisoners. *Journal of Clinical Psychology*, 49, 576-585.

Sheard, Michael H., Marini, James L., Bridges, Carolyn I., and Wagner, Ernest (1976). The Effect of Lithium on Impulsive Aggressive Behavior in Man. *American Journal of Psychiatry*, 133, 1409-1413.

Shepherd, Jade (2016). 'I am very glad and cheered when I hear the flute': The Treatment of Criminal Lunatics in Late Victorian Broadmoor. *Medical History*, 60, 473-491.

Shore, Heather (1999). *Artful Dodgers: Youth and Crime in Early Nineteenth-Century London*. Woodbridge, Suffolk: Royal Historical Society / Boydell Press, Boydell and Brewer.

Sims, Henry Marion (1893). Hystero-Epilepsy: A Report of Seven Cases Cured by Surgical Treatment. *American Journal of Obstetrics and Diseases of Women and Children*, 28, 80-88.

Sinason, Valerie (1992). *Mental Handicap and the Human Condition: New Approaches from the Tavistock*. London: Free Association Books.

Sinason, Valerie (1999). Psychoanalysis and Mental Handicap: Experience from the Tavistock Clinic. In Johan De Groef and Evelyn Heinemann (Eds.). *Psychoanalysis and Mental*

Handicap. Andrew Weller (Transl.), pp. 194-206. London: Free Association Books.

Sinason, Valerie (2010). *Mental Handicap and the Human Condition: An Analytic Approach to Intellectual Disability. Revised Edition.* London: Free Association Books.

Smail, Kenneth (1991). Interview with Jeffrey L. Dahmer. 6th August. Cited in Brian Masters (1993). *The Shrine of Jeffrey Dahmer,* p. 237, n. 3. London: Hodder and Stoughton, and Dunton Green, Sevenoaks, Kent: Hodder and Stoughton, Hodder and Stoughton Limited.

Smith, John M. Powis (1931). *The Origin and History of Hebrew Law.* Chicago, Illinois: University of Chicago Press.

Smith, Maurice Hamblin (1924). The Mental Conditions Found in Certain Sexual Offenders. *The Lancet.* 29th March, pp. 643-646.

Snodgrass, Jon (1984). William Healy (1896-1963): Pioneer Child Psychiatrist and Criminologist. *Journal of the History of the Behavioral Sciences,* 20, 332-339.

Socarides, Charles W. (1959). Meaning and Content of a Pedophiliac Perversion. *Journal of the American Psychoanalytic Association,* 7, 84-94.

Socarides, Charles W. (1988). *The Preoedipal Origin and Psychoanalytic Therapy of Sexual Perversions.* Madison, Connecticut: International Universities Press.

Socarides, Charles W. (1991). Adult-Child Sexual Pairs: Psychoanalytic Findings. *Journal of Psychohistory,* 19, 185-189.

Southwood, Martin (1958). *John Howard: Prison Reformer. An Account of His Life and Travels.* London: Independent Press.

Sperling, Melitta (1959). A Study of Deviate Sexual Behavior in Children by the Method of Simultaneous Analysis of Mother and Child. In Lucie Jessner and Eleanor Pavenstedt (Eds.). *Dynamic Psychopathology in Childhood,* pp. 221-242. New York: Grune and Stratton.

Sperling, Melitta (1978). *Psychosomatic Disorders in Childhood.* Otto E. Sperling (Ed.). New York: Jason Aronson.

Stahl, Stephen M., and Morrissette, Debbi Ann (2014). *Stahl's Illustrated Violence: Neural Circuits, Genetics and Treatment.* Cambridge: Cambridge University Press.

Starchild, Adam (1990). Rape of Youth in Prisons and Juvenile Facilities. *Journal of Psychohistory,* 18, 145-150.

References

Steward, Jill (2012). Travel to the Spas: The Growth of Health Tourism in Central Europe, 1850-1914. In Gemma Blackshaw and Sabine Wieber (Eds.). *Journeys into Madness: Mapping Mental Illness in the Austro-Hungarian Empire*, pp. 72-89. New York: Berghahn Books.

Stewart, Lynn A. (1993). Profile of Female Firesetters: Implications for Treatment. *British Journal of Psychiatry*, 163, 248-256.

Stewart, Pamela Windham (2016a). Interventions with Mothers and Babies in Prisons: Collision of Internal and External Worlds. In Stella Acquarone (Ed.). *Surviving the Early Years: The Importance of Early Intervention with Babies at Risk*, pp. 101-111. London: Karnac Books.

Stewart, Pamela Windham (2016b). Creating Mother and Baby Therapy Groups in Prison: Emotional Valuation. *Psychoanalytic Psychotherapy*, 30, 152-163.

Stewart, Pamela Windham (2019). Twenty Years in Prison: Reflections on the Birth of the Born Inside Project and Psychotherapy in HMP Holloway. In Pamela Windham Stewart and Jessica Collier (Eds.). *The End of the Sentence: Psychotherapy with Female Offenders*, pp. 23-40. London: Routledge / Taylor and Francis Group, and Abingdon, Oxfordshire: Routledge / Taylor and Francis Group.

Strauss, Eric B. (1939). Psycho-Therapy in Prison. *Howard Journal*, 5, 166-168.

Stroud, William (1847). *A Treatise on the Physical Cause of the Death of Christ, and its Relation to the Principles and Practice of Christianity.* London: Hamilton and Adams.

Swain, John (n.d.). *The Pleasures of the Torture Chamber.* London: Noel Douglas.

Taylor, Alfred Swaine (1905). *The Principles and Practice of Medical Jurisprudence: Fifth Edition. Vol. I.* Frederick J. Smith (Ed.). London: J. and A. Churchill.

Taylor, Karen J. (1985). Venereal Disease in Nineteenth-Century Children. *Journal of Psychohistory*, 12, 431-463.

Taylor, Pamela J. (1985). Motives for Offending Among Violent and Psychotic Men. *British Journal of Psychiatry*, 147, 491-498.

Terranova, Claudio, and Rocca, Gabriele (2016). Homicide Committed by Psychiatric Patients: Psychiatrists' Liability in Italian Law Cases. *Medicine, Science and the Law*, 56, 58-64.

References

Theobald, Henry Studdy (1924). *The Law Relating to Lunacy*. London: Stevens and Sons.

Thomson, J. Bruce (1870a). The Hereditary Nature of Crime. *Journal of Mental Science*, 15, 487-498.

Thomson, J. Bruce (1870b). The Psychology of Criminals. *Journal of Mental Science*, 16, 321-350.

Tuke, Daniel Hack (1885). Case of Moral Insanity or Congenital Moral Defect, with Commentary. *Journal of Mental Science*, 31, 360-366.

van Leeuwen, Mirjam E., and Harte, Joke M. (2017). Violence Against Mental Health Care Professionals: Prevalence, Nature and Consequences. *Journal of Forensic Psychiatry and Psychology*, 28, 581-598.

Victoria (1872). Journal Entry. 29th February, pp. 197-198. In Extracts from the Queen's Journal. In Victoria (1926). *The Letters of Queen Victoria: Second Series. A Selection from Her Majesty's Correspondence and Journal Between the Years 1862 and 1878. Published by Authority of His Majesty the King. In Two Volumes. Vol. II. 1870-1878.* George Earle Buckle (Ed.), pp. 197-200. London: John Murray.

Vizard, Eileen (1997). Adolescents Who Sexually Abuse. In Estela V. Welldon and Cleo Van Velsen (Eds.). *A Practical Guide to Forensic Psychotherapy*, pp. 48-55. London: Jessica Kingsley Publishers.

Vizard, Eileen; Monck, Elizabeth, and Misch, Peter (1995). Child and Adolescent Sex Abuse Perpetrators: A Review of the Research Literature. *Journal of Child Psychology and Psychiatry and Allied Disciplines*, 36, 731-756.

Vizard, Eileen; Wynick, Sarah; Hawkes, Colin; Woods, John, and Jenkins, Jill (1996). Juvenile Sex Offenders: Assessment Issues. *British Journal of Psychiatry*, 168, 259-262.

von Krafft-Ebing, Richard (1895). *Nervosität und neurasthenische Zustände*. In Hermann Nothnagel (Ed.). *Specielle Pathologie und Therapie: XII. Band, II. Theil. Nervosität und neurasthenische Zustände von Prof. Dr. R. v. Krafft-Ebing*, pp. [v]-210. Vienna: Alfred Holder.

von Winterstein, Alfred Freiherr (1912). Zur Psychoanalyse des Reisens. *Imago*, 1, 489-506.

Walker, Zuzana, and Seifert, Ruth (1994). Violent Incidents in a Psychiatric Intensive Care Unit. *British Journal of Psychiatry*, 164, 826-828.

References

Welch, Katherine E. (2007). *The Roman Amphitheatre: From its Origins to the Colosseum*. Cambridge: Cambridge University Press.

Welldon, Estela (n.d. [1985]). Application of Group Analytic Psychotherapy to Those with Sexual Perversions. In Terence E. Lear (Ed.). *Spheres of Group Analysis*, pp. 96-108. n.p.: n.p.

Welldon, Estela V. (1988). *Mother, Madonna, Whore: The Idealization and Denigration of Motherhood*. London: Free Association Books.

Welldon, Estela V. (1991). Psychology and Psychopathology in Women: A Psychoanalytic Perspective. *British Journal of Psychiatry*, 158, Supplement 10, 85-92.

Welldon, Estela V. (1993). Forensic Psychotherapy and Group Analysis. *Group Analysis*, 26, 487-502.

Welldon, Estela V. (1996). Contrasts in Male and Female Sexual Perversions. In Christopher Cordess and Murray Cox (Eds.). *Forensic Psychotherapy: Crime, Psychodynamics and the Offender Patient. Volume II. Mainly Practice*, pp. 273-289. London: Jessica Kingsley Publishers.

Welldon, Estela (2001). Babies as Transitional Objects. In Brett Kahr (Ed.). *Forensic Psychotherapy and Psychopathology: Winnicottian Perspectives*, pp. 19-25. London: H. Karnac (Books).

Welldon, Estela V. (2011). *Playing with Dynamite: A Personal Approach to the Psychoanalytic Understanding of Perversions, Violence, and Criminality*. London: Karnac Books.

Welldon, Estela (2012). Couples Who Kill: The Malignant Bonding. In John Adlam, Anne Aiyegbusi, Pam Kleinot, Anna Motz, and Christopher Scanlon (Eds.). *The Therapeutic Milieu Under Fire: Security and Insecurity in Forensic Mental Health*, pp. 162-172. London: Jessica Kingsley Publishers.

Welldon, Estela (2015). Forensic Psychotherapy. *Psychoanalytic Psychotherapy*, 29, 211-227.

Whyte, Frederic (1925a). *The Life of W.T. Stead: In Two Volumes. Vol. I*. London: Jonathan Cape, and New York: Houghton Mifflin Company.

Whyte, Frederic (1925b). *The Life of W.T. Stead: In Two Volumes. Vol. II*. London: Jonathan Cape, and New York: Houghton Mifflin Company.

Wieser, Stefan (1972). Psychiatrische Therapie, Möglichkeiten und Grenzen. In Hans Göppinger and Hermann Witter (Eds.). *Handbuch der forensischen Psychiatrie I: Teil A. Die rechtlichen*

References

Grundlagen. Teil B. Die psychiatrischen Grundlagen, pp. 810-854. Berlin: Springer-Verlag.

Wilks-Wiffen, Stephanie (2011). *Voice of a Child*. London: Howard League for Penal Reform. The Howard League for Penal Reform. [https://howardleague.org/wp-content/uploads/2018/05/Voice-of-a-Child.pdf; Accessed on 9th March, 2019].

Winnicott, Donald W. (1943). Delinquency Research. *New Era in Home and School*, 24, 65-67.

Winnicott, Donald W. (1945). The Return of the Evacuated Child. In Donald W. Winnicott (1957). *The Child and the Outside World: Studies in Developing Relationships*. Janet Hardenberg (Ed.), pp. 88-92. London: Tavistock Publications.

Winnicott, Donald W. (1949). Letter to S.H. Hodge. 1st September. In Donald W. Winnicott (1987). *The Spontaneous Gesture: Selected Letters of D.W. Winnicott*. F. Robert Rodman (Ed.), pp. 17-19. Cambridge, Massachusetts: Harvard University Press.

Winnicott, Donald W. (1956). The Antisocial Tendency. In Donald W. Winnicott (1958). *Collected Papers: Through Paediatrics to Psycho-Analysis*, pp. 306-315. London: Tavistock Publications.

Winnicott, Donald W. (1968). Delinquency as a Sign of Hope. *Prison Service Journal*, 7, Number 27, 2-7.

Winnicott, Donald W., and Britton, Clare (1944). The Problem of Homeless Children. *New Era in Home and School*, 25, 155-161.

Winnicott, Donald W., and Britton, Clare (1947). Residential Management as Treatment for Difficult Children: The Evolution of a Wartime Hostels Scheme. *Human Relations*, 1, 87-97.

Woods, John (1997). Breaking the Cycle of Abuse and Abusing: Individual Psychotherapy for Juvenile Sex Offenders. *Clinical Child Psychology and Psychiatry*, 2, 379-392.

Woodward, Samuel B. (1845). Homicidal Impulse. *American Journal of Insanity*, 1, 323-326.

Wortis, Joseph (1934). Diary Entry. 1st November. In Joseph Wortis (1954). *Fragments of an Analysis with Freud*, pp. 54-59. New York: Simon and Schuster.

Wray, George A., and Eldridge, Harold W. (1970). A Knife Swallowed in Prison Retrieved at Oesophagoscopy. *Medicine Science and the Law*, 10, 85.

Yang, Yaling; Raine, Adrian; Narr, Katherine L., Colletti, Patrick, and

References

Toga, Arthur W. (2009). Localization of Deformations within the Amygdala in Individuals with Psychopathy. *Archives of General Psychiatry,* 66, 986-994.

Yukhnenko, Denis; Sridhar, Shivpriya, and Fazel, Seena (2019). A Systematic Review of Criminal Recidivism Rates Worldwide: 3-Year Update. *Wellcome Open Research,* 4:28, 1-12. Wellcome Open Research. https://wellcomeopenresearch.org/articles/4-28 (Accessed 22nd April 2020).

Zilboorg, Gregory (1931). Translator's Note. In Franz Alexander and Hugo Staub. *The Criminal, the Judge, and the Public: A Psychological Analysis.* Gregory Zilboorg (Transl.), pp. v-x. New York: Macmillan Company.

INDEX

Index

Index

Index

Index

Index

Index

Index

Index

Index

Sadism, 6, 10, 12, 16, 20, 86, 105, 112, 117, 149
Salivary testosterone, 98
Sanborn, Alanson, 94
Schizophrenia, 2, 4, 32, 83
Schreiber, Flora Rheta, 103-104, 108-109
Second World War, 56, 140
Secondary paedophilia, 82-83
Secondary sexual characteristics, 78
Section on Forensic Psychiatry, American Psychiatric Association, Washington, D.C., U.S.A., 59
Secure institutions, 128, 135
Sedatives, 116
Seduction, 72, 153
Self-defence, 123
Self-hatred, 79
Self-loathing, 79
Self-mutilation, 128
Seneca, Lucius Annaeus, 15
Separation, 56, 80, 133, 140, 144
Separation trauma, 80
Serial killing, 96, 103, 122, 123
Sexual abuse, 42, 64-91, 102, 110, 117, 119, 122, 129, 142, 146, 153-154
Sexual assault, *see* Sexual violence
Sexual fantasies, 43, 65-66, 83, 124
Sexual intercourse, 68, 83, 106
Sexual molestation, *see* Sexual abuse
Sexual offending, 42, 65, 69, 70, 71, 72, 75, 76, 77, 79, 81, 87, 88, 90, 131, 140
Sexual perversions, *see* Perversions
Sexual violence, 8, 72
Sexual voyeurism, *see* Voyeurism

Sexualisation, 64, 87
Sexually transmitted diseases, 68
Shakespeare, William, 11, 39-40, 135, 150, 152-153
Shame, 16, 39, 104, 106, 107, 110, 111, 112, 119, 120, 121
Shaming, 16, 107, 110, 112, 119
Sheppard, William Dillon, 67
Shooting, 1, 4-5, 6, 16, 42, 93, 94, 109, 111, 119
Sibling abuse, 7-8, 42, 72-73, 86, 111-112, 153-154
Siblings, 7, 72, 86, 103, 111, 112, 143, 152, 153
Sinason, Valerie, 137
Sing Sing Prison, Ossining, New York, U.S.A., 75
Slavery, 35, 130
Slaying by sword, 15
Slicing, 15
Smith, Maurice Hamblin, 54, 69
Socarides, Charles, 77-81, 82
Social psychology, 98
Sodomy, 67, 101
Solitary confinement, 129
Solon, 152
Special psychiatric hospital, 7
Sperling, Melitta, 86-87
Splitting, 80
St. Bartholomew's Hospital, London, 138
St. Elizabeths Hospital, Washington, D.C., U.S.A., 73
Stabbing, 106, 119, 120, 129
Staffordshire, England, 132
Starvation, 16
State Lunatic Asylum, Worcester, Massachusetts, U.S.A., 93-94
State Society of Judges and Barristers, Budapest, Hungary,

Index

Index

Violent fantasies, 39, 40-41, 66
Visual hallucinations, *see*
    Hallucinations
Vitae Parallelae (Lucius Mestrius
    Plutarch), 152
Vizard, Eileen, 87-88, 89, 140
von Winterstein, Alfred Freiherr, 46
Voyeurism, 134-135

Wales, 69
"Warrior gene", 98
Weaning, 73-74
Weihofen, Henry, 76
Welldon, Estela Valentina, 61-62,
    63, 85, 137
West Midlands, England, 132
Whipping, 144
White, William Alanson, 60
"Wilhelm", 111, 112
"William B.", 7-8
Winnicott, Donald W., 55, 56-58,
    59

Wisconsin State Fair, Wisconsin
    State Fair Park, West Allis,
    Wisconsin, U.S.A., 112
Wittels, Fritz, 45-46
Woodward, Samuel, 93-94
World Health Organization,
    Geneva, Switzerland, 58
Wortis, Joseph, 44
Wright, David Minton, 94-95

"Yannis", 124-125
"Yorkshire Ripper", *see* Sutcliffe,
    Peter
Young Abusers Project, Tavistock
    Clinic Foundation, Child and
    Family Department, Tavistock
    Clinic, Tavistock Centre,
    Tavistock and Portman N.H.S.
    Trust, Belsize Park, London,
    87-88, 89

Zhou dynasty, 15
Ziferstein, Isadore, 52